JUMP-STARTS

FOR
THOUGHTFUL MEDITATION

Power to You,
Oct. 18

75 SUPERCHARGED TOPICS
BY CALVIN S. METCALF

Calvin S Metcalf

Printed by
Publishing and Printing, Inc.
Knoxville, Tennessee

This book is dedicated to the faithful members of Central Baptist Church of Fountain City, Knoxville, Tennessee. For over twenty years these dear people have been giving me "Jump-starts for Thoughtful Meditation." Every word of encouragement has been stored away and now has culminated in this book.

ACKNOWLEDGMENTS

My deepest appreciation goes to my wife Bobbie who gave me valuable input on every aspect of this book, and to Robin Rosser for editing, typesetting, and proofreading. Karen J. Wilson and Linda McNeil also served in a support role. I am likewise grateful for all who have encouraged me to give my writings a larger readership.

CONTENTS

PREFACE

The word "jump-start" means "to receive energy from another source." The picture is that of jumper cables stretching from a car with a live battery pumping energy into a car with a dead battery. In many ways this is a parable of our life in Christ. We who are dead in our trespasses and our sins have need of life from another source. Our Lord Jesus has come to pump new energy into our beings. He comes again and again through His Holy Spirit to recharge our batteries of faith and keep us in the fellowship of His love.

The use of the word "jump-starts" for this book describes its purpose. It is designed to give the reader some ideas for thoughtful meditation. Included are many topics with short comments. The point is not to say everything that can be said on a subject, but to say enough to stimulate some thoughtful connections with God.

The fact that God has created us with a capacity to repent means we are spiritually rechargeable. Even though we often become lifeless, we can become rejuvenated. We have not sinned away our chance for personal progress. There is always a place to begin again. We do not have to stay the way we are. Our greatest hope is in the fact we can grow in the grace and knowledge of our Lord Jesus Christ.

Jump-starts for Thoughtful Meditation is divided into the following three divisions: (1) Godly Connections, (2) People Power, and (3) Personal Voltage. These divisions are designed to offer some helpful thoughts about God, about others, and about ourselves.

- PART ONE -
GODLY CONNECTIONS

*"Yours, O Lord, is the greatness and the power and
the glory and the majesty and the splendor....In your
hands are strength and power to exalt and give
strength to all."*
I Chronicles 29:11-12 (NIV)

- ONE -
FAITH CONNECTION

What is our advantage as Christians? Do we have a special protection from the pains and penalties of life? Is ours a special standing before God as though He gives us favored treatment? Are we somehow exempt from war, pestilence, famine, and disease?

The answer is "no" because life does not seem to have favorites. It tends to rain misfortune and blessings upon the just as well as the unjust.

We do have an advantage as Christians, however, and our advantage is that in the midst of tribulation, distress, persecution, famine, nakedness, peril, or sword we are more than conquerors. God meets us in the rut of our own agonies to show us who we are. He inspires our perseverance. He tutors us through our trauma. He gives us a reason to believe in ourselves and those who meet us in the valley of our tears. He magnifies the meaning of grace even though healing might never happen.

Our advantage is not some mysterious rescue. It is a powerful Presence from which there is no separation. Paul reminds us that none of the troublesome things of life can ever separate us from the love of God in Christ Jesus our Lord. In fact, we are not exempt from them; we are blessed through them.

Sometimes it takes these things to help us discover the love we have. Even though most times we make the very hell we live in, He wants to meet us in the lowest moments of our lives. Whatever disease and despair may wish to conquer us, He reminds us that we are not far from Him.

Of course, there are times when God appears to be silent and absent. Our prayers for a "quick fix" or a dramatic intervention seem to fall on deaf ears. Our childish concept of a God who will rescue us in every difficulty disappoints us. We want to shake our fist at God and cry, "Unfair, unfair!"

But then in the midst of our most painful moment we discover a peace that is unexplainable. We find an unconquerable reason for faith and hope. We experience a grave-defying assurance that even the "valley of the shadow of death" is crossable. It is as though our most troubling moments usher us into a meeting place with God.

No, He does not put us there. He finds us there, and we are conditioned to receive Him there. Our advantage is simply this: nothing--and that means *nothing*--can separate us from the love of God. Faith connects us to that kind of hope.

- TWO -
A WORSHIP THOUGHT

Public worship is an interesting phenomenon of our spiritual lives. It has about as many definitions as there are people in attendance. There are hundreds of needs within a given congregation. How can a handful of worship leaders meet everyone's expectations in a brief time of worship?

They can't. The Holy Spirit has to translate and communicate. Truth has to be internalized. Music has to be appropriated into our emotional being. Prayers have to be composed by everyone. We invoke God's spirit upon us and unless we allow Him to have our undivided attention, worship becomes little more than a few moments of boring spectatorship. Worship is something in which God participates. In fact, it is not worship unless He does.

Should we always expect people to come to church with something as serious as God on their minds? Should it be made easier for the Holy Spirit to capture their attention? Should we lure folk with some kind of gimmick and then zap them with God? Is it too much to expect people nowadays to hunger and thirst for righteousness? Must we first serve an appetizer or perhaps a preview of coming attractions? Has God lost His appeal? Do we need the ways of the world to give Him secular creditability? What is worship to the person who does not consider himself or herself spiritual?

Worship is an event that gets something going between God and the worshiper. It introduces the living God in such a way that His unconditional love is obvious and His understanding of life's pain provides hope.

Public worship does not happen in a vacuum. It occurs in the context of people. There is a sense of belonging and being identified with the people of God. We are conscious of others and others are conscious of us. Worship is as public as everyone singing together, but as private as one's personal pilgrimage. If God is sought He can design a blessing to meet everyone's particular need.

What a call to worship when the psalmist said, "I was glad when they said unto me, let us go into the house of the Lord"! May it be so for us today as we yield our minds to God's truth, our hearts to His love, and our lives to His great commission.

- THREE -
IT'S A MIRACLE!

A miracle is not a miracle until its source has been recognized. A beautiful sunset loses much of its splendor without a grasp of Who causes it to happen. The dawning of a new day is a spectacular event for all who see the divine paintbrush at work. Life is dull and routine if there is no awareness of God's intervention in its particulars.

Every day is full of mystery and meaning. The miraculous is as common as the explainable. The journey of life is one of faith. It requires us to see beyond the natural to the supernatural. Most of life is lived in the context of that which we do not fully understand. We simply trust the process.

What, then, is a miracle? A miracle is any aspect of life that has God written all over it. It is not only that which is humanly unexplainable. It is that which has redemptive consequences for us. It is outside our ability to achieve. It is grace in motion as God's power to perform is recognized.

A miracle is capable of many interpretations. All of us do not see the same miracles. They are individualized to minister to our unique circumstances. We must not minimize each other's miracles simply because we have a different interpretation to some event. Surely it would be a form of blasphemy to ridicule that which another person feels is God's involvement in his or her life.

We are blessed indeed when we can behold the hand of God at work in His world. When the miracles of life leap out at us in unexpected moments, we can surely praise God for His unmistakable presence. A miracle is not a miracle for us until we have some significant way to celebrate its occurrence.

We do not announce every miracle as though we have a more favored position with God. A powerful personal miracle is a humbling experience, and we savor the event only for God's glory. Sometimes it is a moment of grace for private interpretation only. Then again it may be an occasion for others to join the celebration.

Let us be mindful of life's miracles and find ways to share God's power for God's glory.

- FOUR -
THUS SAITH THE LORD

How do we know when God has spoken? How can we tell if something we read or hear is inspired by God? What are the criteria by which we determine if our thoughts have divine approval? Do we always know when we do what we do that we are on God's mission?

Perhaps the will of God is never as simple as we would like to make it. Having a religious thought or doing something in the name of the church does not necessarily mean God inspired it. Jesus made it clear that not everyone who said "Lord, Lord" would enter the kingdom. We must somehow test our inspirations to see if they are of God. But that is precisely our question. How do we know when God has spoken?

Sometimes we have to think and say and do the best we know and hope that time will prove God was motivating us. The will of God is a walk of faith. We are not given a daily script. We make up our lines as we go along in faith believing God inspires us on the journey.

To live as though we have it all together and know all there is to know is to be obnoxiously naive. Life at its best is always being open to the variety of ways in which God may speak. Most often our assurance comes from looking back and seeing the hand of God in the road just traveled. It gives us courage to face the road ahead. It equips us to listen for what "thus saith the Lord" in every circumstance.

It is doubtful that Paul said to his Roman guard one day that he was going to write a book in the Bible. He didn't know. Yet, he did sit down and write a letter to the beloved believers at Philippi. When they read it they said, "God has spoken. This letter from Paul is indeed a letter from God." Other churches received the same. Therefore, they saved many of his letters and shared them among the churches, and their collection forms a significant part of our New Testament today.

The point is, God has spoken, God is speaking, and God will continue to speak. The most pertinent question may not be How do we know? but, Will we listen? God's voice may not always ring from the rafters of the sanctuary, but may come from the still small voice of the workplace. We may struggle for it in our quiet place of prayer and meditation, yet find it in our service to others. There is no formula to guarantee we will always know when God has spoken. But we will know and we will find Him if we search for Him with all our hearts.

- FIVE -
IN STEP WITH GOD

Walking with God is a beautiful way of describing our Christian pilgrimage. In our walk with the Lord we sometimes walk ahead of Him. We become impatient with His slower pace and move on with what we assume is a better gait toward our goal. It is more like a race with God than a walk. We rush to conclusions. We hurry up our prayers. Rather than wait for clearer signals we compose our own agenda for the living of our days. In our haste to get where we are going we want God to quickly bless our plans.

Walking ahead of God we tend to get exhausted. Because we do not wait upon the Lord we do not "mount up on wings as eagles." We do not run without getting weary and we grow faint in our walk. Like children who refuse to hold their parent's hand at a busy intersection, we expose ourselves to a lot of danger when we get ahead of God.

There are also times in our walk with the Lord that we walk behind Him. We drag our feet. We lose interest in the things of God. Our affection becomes focused on things of the world. The church and our Christian witness become a burden rather than a lift. We take out our disappointment with people on God. When He doesn't fix every problem to our liking we withdraw. We do a little spiritual pouting.

Even though we straggle far behind we want to keep Him in sight. We hear Him calling us onward and upward, but somehow the demands of a closer walk are too much. We give passive respect rather than passionate devotion in our walk with God.

Furthermore, there are times when in our walk with the Lord we walk all over Him. We trample His grace. We take advantage of His goodness. We expect Him to be merciful, yet we are cruel. We expect Him to forgive our trespasses, but we refuse to forgive those who trespass against us. We want the benefits of His blessing and His church without making a commitment to either. We want God, but we want Him on our own terms. We stomp around Calvary and wonder why He does not come down from the cross and save us from the discomfort of having to identify with His death. Perhaps we want what God offers more than we want God.

Let us, therefore, not walk ahead of God. Let us not walk behind God. Neither let us walk all over God. Let us walk with God at the pace He chooses.

- SIX -
LOVING GOD

One of the most obvious requirements of the Christian life is that we love God. From the beginning of time it seems evident that God created us in His own image to love us and in turn be loved by us. Yet the most piercing question is, How do we love God? What does it mean to love God with all our heart, mind, and being? How do we know we are loving God to the best of our ability?

These are questions we need to ponder because they are at the heart of what it means to be a Christian person. Perhaps there are three ways in which we can monitor our love for God. By evaluating our feelings, our thoughts, and our actions we can understand what God really means to us.

Since we are emotional beings we are equipped to feel the presence of God. There will be occasions when we will deeply sense His goodness and grace. His comforting assurance will guide us through difficult situations. We will be impressed by things too wonderful to explain. There will be times when the beauty of creation and the evidence of divine handiwork will overwhelm us. At such times we will celebrate our existence. The fact that we are alive and aware of life's privileges and responsibilities gives us a reason to praise God. It may express itself with tears or laughter. Deep down, however, where words do not reach, we know we love God.

We are also intelligent beings capable of thinking God's thoughts after Him. Our involvement with God includes our minds. Our faith commitment is cerebral. We are admonished to study and meditate upon the deeper things of God. Shallow thinking leads to superstition and fear. Integrity of thought leads us to the truth that sets us free. When the lightbulbs of learning God's will and ways are turned on in our minds we celebrate His revelations. As our knowledge increases we discover how much we really love God with all our mind.

Perhaps the hardest expression of our love for God is in our actions. It is difficult at times to put our deep feelings and thoughts into our daily behavior. We feel and know far more than we do. Our strong emotional and mental attachment to God does not always find expression in the way we treat our neighbor. When it does, however, there is a completeness to our love for God which blesses us with great satisfaction.

Thus, we conclude that love for God is not one-dimensional. It is more than emotional spasms, intellectual gymnastics, or outward acts of superficial piety. Authentic love for God comes when every aspect of our being harmonizes in singing, "My Jesus, I love Thee, I know Thou art mine."

- SEVEN -
"AMAZABLE"

A preschooler had just finished her first week ever of Vacation Bible School. Apparently it had been a good experience. She told her mother it was "amazable." Now, adults may smile at the use of such a word, but to a child caught up in the excitement of learning about God it was a beautiful way to express it. She probably said more than she understood. Nonetheless, she found a way to describe a profound happening in her young life.

How long has it been since you had an "amazable" event in your life? How long has it been since you needed to invent a word to describe something that ordinary words do not cover?

It is always good for us from time to time to have an "amazable" experience. It is imperative that we have some blessed events come our way lest we become morbidly pessimistic. Life is filled with too many complicated issues. There is often mystery without meaning, problem without solution, and heartache without comfort. Tragedy, sorrow, and death take their toll upon us. As we move closer and closer to our final destiny we need some "amazable" things to cheer us on our way. It is not easy being human. Without some unexplainable joy overtaking us on the journey we could easily give up in hopeless despair.

Sometimes we may miss that which is "amazable." We turn a corner and there is God as big as life. If we fail to celebrate and share such an encounter it may have little or no effect upon us. The small light that shines into the darkness of our despair is better than no light at all. The more we focus upon it the brighter it glows to dispel the blackness that may surround us. Friends who come our way in times of need may not overwhelm us, yet they are "amazable" in the way they can help heal our hurts. Sin may overtake us and guilt may unmercifully whip us, but grace is God's "amazable" reaction. He forgives the repentant and encourages the wayward to sin no more.

Love is an "amazable" ingredient of life. The capacity to care and to be cared for are often unexplainable, undeserved, and "amazable." Being alive is "amazable" when we consider the fragile nature of our existence. Let us, therefore, never get too old to look through childish eyes and discover that which is "amazable."

- EIGHT -
ASSUMED GOODNESS

Do you think sometimes we tend to substitute our own goodness for God? We worship our value system instead of the One who gave it to us. We look down on those who have not arrived at our spiritual status. While thanking God we are not like other sinners, we forget that "all of us have sinned and come short of the glory of God." We fret about those who interrupt our devotions. We are irritated with worship when our standards are violated by sermons, songs, prayers, and programs which are not to our liking. Our witness and ministry focus upon our need to reproduce other Christians just like ourselves. We have our own preconceived notions of what life is all about. We are unbending toward any other way of seeing things. We worship at the shrine of our own intelligence. Our god is limited to what we think, what we do, and what we say. We have created a god in our own image rather than looking to the God who created us in His image. How easy it is to turn the vehicles of our faith into instruments of an acceptable idolatry.

How do we keep our assumed goodness from being our God? How do we avoid the pitfalls of a synthetic religiosity? For one thing, we struggle to keep our faith in Jesus personal and vital. We dare not let our commitment to Christ become nothing more than religious routine. We monitor our convictions lest they become mere guidelines for our own private religious club. We work at finding ways of being in the world but not of the world. We expand the horizons of our hope by believing in the redeemability of all people. We relax in the freedom that everyone need not have our particular experience. As Jesus said, "There are other sheep which are not of this fold."

We grow to see that God is bigger than anything we think or say or do. He alone is the focus of our praise and the impetus of our witness. We are not called to save people by ourselves, but to introduce them to a saving God. It may go something like this-- "God, this is Bill, who has some needs only You can meet. Bill, this is God, who loves you so much that He gave His only Son that you might believe and have everlasting life." As we let go and let God have His way, our goodness fades into His greatness. He then becomes Lord of lords and King of kings to others in His own special way.

- NINE -
SOUL RESTORED

The reality of sin and our susceptibility to its power often create the necessity for spiritual recovery. Time and again we find ourselves inundated by iniquity with an awesome hangover of guilt. Life has a way of wearing down our resistance and we succumb to those temptations which appeal to our weaknesses. How often we are faced with a need to be forgiven and to have the cobwebs of careless living cleansed from our souls.

We are blessed indeed when we recognize the extent of our transgressions and have the will to let our Lord deliver us from evil. The gospel reminds us that we do not have to stay the way we are. We can become more than what we have been. The discomfort of sin can become an avenue of grace through repentance and faith.

After all, spiritual recovery is what the Christian faith is all about. We come to Jesus not because we are so good, but because we want to be. If we were perfect specimens of righteous living we would have no need for the Christ of God to deliver us from all that hinders and oppresses us. If our love were pure we would never need to struggle with hostile feelings. If our words were always kind and our deeds were always helpful we would never need to say "I'm sorry." If our faith were even as a grain of mustard seed the mountains of adversity would seem like a peaceful valley.

Because God is not as real to us as we often pretend, we drift into periods of indifference and iniquity. Our sin separates us from the people and the resources which remind us of God's healing grace. Therefore, the message of our faith is a reminder to ourselves and to all who have sinned that spiritual recovery is not only possible, but is God's dream for all humankind.

The shepherd psalmist expressed it well when he wrote, "He restoreth my soul." Anyone who has ever walked and talked with God as the psalmist is aware of God's restoring power. It is this consciousness of God's will to save which enables us to survive the wiles of the devil. We are not mentally nor spiritually equipped to handle our sins all by ourselves. Unless we are open to God's restoration we are lost in our sins.

Indeed our hope is in Him who said, "Come unto me all ye who labor and are heavy laden and I will give you rest." "All who come to me I will in no wise cast out." Properly responding to these kind of promises will enable us to say with the psalmist, "He restoreth my soul."

- TEN -
GOD'S PROMISED ETERNITY

The mystery of time is surpassed only by the mystery of eternity. Time as we know it has beginning and end. It has definable boundaries. Eternity has no beginning and no end. Because we live in time we are conditioned by the limitations of that which is temporary and perishable. Our thought processes are not equipped to think in terms of that which is everlasting and eternal. We reach into that realm of existence by faith. It is the vision of the heart and the eyes of the soul which look into the land of forever and ever. We search for words because our vocabularies are limited as we try to discuss that which is timeless. "Infinity" is a word we seldom use because we know so little about it.

The scriptures give us a hint of heaven, yet the only thing we know for sure about it is we shall be with God. Of course that is enough, but our exploring minds try to envision what heaven will be like. We finger lovingly those passages which contain vision and suggestion about the hereafter. Although Bible writers used earth's most precious objects to describe heaven, we still live with the reality that it has not entered human minds all God has in store for His people.

However, this does not mean we should give no thought to that which is eternal. It is important to let our imaginations explore that which is immortal. It stretches our minds to reflect upon that which is ultimate. It is a matter of faith that we have any interest at all in God's promised eternity. Indifference about everlasting life most likely reveals a carelessness about earthly life. The point to ponder is the awesome relation between the two. We go on living in the hereafter on the basis of how we live in the here and now. There is an eternal dimension to life that we do well not to ignore even though it surpasses our most disciplined thoughts.

We must never let a lazy mentality keep us from looking deep into the mysteries of whatever lies before us. While living in time, let us, therefore, look beyond the temporal to that which is permanent and eternal. It is another way to reflect upon God and His glory.

- ELEVEN -
MORE THAN LUCK

There are a lot of things in life which seem to happen with little or no explanation. We tend to call such occurrences "luck," and if they seem to defy the laws of mere chance we call them "miracles." Most of life's unexplainable events are put in one of these categories. "Luck" is often seen as the result of mere coincidence while "miracle" has providential implication. Luck can be either good or bad depending on how it affects us. The chain of events which we call "good fortune" is seldom attributed to God. Yet, when things go bad we want to blame God or some fate that has dealt us an unkind blow.

The question is, Will we go through life trusting our luck or trusting God? If our commitment is only to luck then we have a fickle god. Luck can turn against us and wreak havoc in our lives. It is like the country song which says, "If it weren't for bad luck I'd have no luck at all." Life is full of just as many sad coincidences as happy ones.

We live on an emotional roller coaster when all we have to lean on is luck. We cannot trust life in this sinful world always to be fair. No matter how good we try to be, some folk will lie about us, turn on us and hurt us in any number of ways. Although some events can be kind to us, others can be cruel. Sooner or later luck will run out on us.

This is why we need to put our trust in something, or might we say *Someone*, more substantial than mere luck. It is helpful to recognize a series of events that might bring us a period of good fortune. It is tragic, however, when we lose sight of God in all our circumstances. He joins in the celebration of our successes and steadies us in the midst of our failures. He creates within us a trusting spirit so that whatever life imposes upon us of goodwill or bad we know a loving God continues to reign supreme. The only way we can really consider ourselves lucky is that someone, sometime, introduced us to Jesus and we embraced His life-giving grace.

- TWELVE -
LORD OF THE LOSERS

One of the most redemptive discoveries in life is that we are never nearer God than when we need Him. The scriptures seem to reveal God as One who gravitates toward helpless, hurting humanity. In Egypt, He heard the cry of people in bondage. The psalmist made a case for God's nearness in times of fear and distress. The prophets saw humility as a prerequisite for the godly walk. Jesus, while on earth, found acceptance and identity with people whose lives, for the most part, had "bottomed out." The prodigal son, who had come to the end of his rope in the far country, was of great concern to the father. Tax collectors and a variety of sinners were the object of Jesus' affection. The lepers, the lame, the blind, and the mentally deranged were candidates for our Lord's compassion. It bothered scribes and Pharisees that one who claimed to be the Son of God had little to do with the religious establishment.

It must surely be at the point of need that God converges upon our lives. It would appear that God is allergic to those who flaunt their righteousness and personal victories. He will not tolerate those who gloat in ungodly success. He is Lord of the losers. He reaches out to those who have lost their reasons to be proud. He comforts those whose sorrow has produced some tears of repentance. He heals those whose hurt has taught them to be kind and redemptive. He forgives those whose painful guilt has given them a forgiving disposition. He wants us to do unto others as we would have Him do unto us.

Often it takes a broken spirit and a contrite heart to understand how near God wants to be to us and how near He wants us to be to one another. Perhaps the key to a life of genuine happiness is to grasp the greatness of our needs. He or she who has no need for friends will not be friendly. He or she who has no need of God will not be godly. Of a truth, the songwriter wrote, "Just when I need Him most, Jesus is near to comfort and cheer, just when I need Him most."

- THIRTEEN -
GOD'S REPUTATION

There is an interesting dimension to our Christian commitment in which we feel it is our duty to make God look good. We are forever trying to explain the unexplainable in ways that will protect God's reputation. Somehow we feel the pressure to defend Him who needs no defense. If we pray for something that does not occur, rather than accept its denial by faith, our humanistic tendency is to give it some kind of interpretation. We will rationalize and spiritualize until we are sure God is relieved of all responsibility for not answering our prayer.

The truth of the matter is that God does not heal everyone for whom we pray. He does not give us everything we ask, even though it seems so consistent with who He is. Our greatest discovery may be that we do not know why. Our greatest expressions of humility may come from accepting the fact that His ways are not our ways and His thoughts are not our thoughts.

God does not require us to be His public relations experts. He calls us to be a servant people. We defend the way He is by the gentle way we live and serve. We have no argument for God other than the love He has shed abroad in our hearts. No amount of logical debate can take the place of a spirit-controlled temperament.

It might just be that in our attempt to defend God, we are actually trying to defend our own preconceived notions about God. We have theories to defend and concepts to protect which may have very little to do with the living, loving God we all must serve and worship. God will do quite well for Himself if we will allow His presence to prevail in the honest pursuit of His truth.

God always looks bad when we who claim to be His followers become angry and hateful in His defense. He looks best when we permit the things which break His heart to create within us a sense of similar brokenness. We serve Him best who reflect His gracious spirit in everything we say and do. The most precious commodity in advertising God is grace. He has no other means of defense. Neither should we.

- FOURTEEN -
GOD'S ASSIGNMENT

Sometimes we treat the gospel with a mild courtesy rather than with the radical commitment it requires. We enjoy its story and respect its truth, but we are cautious about personal application. On the surface we applaud its proclamation without considering the depth of its implications. Preaching becomes a kind of spiritual entertainment rather than a serious call to action. Many hear sermons on salvation but reject God's grace. We praise stewardship messages but continue to mock the offering plate with the absence of our tithes.

We marvel over the eloquence of those who preach about social issues, yet we keep most of our prejudices intact. We weep over the missionary stories from foreign lands, yet we never have the same emotion concerning the homeless, hungry, and lost within our own community. We love to hear the story of God's grace and goodness toward us, yet we are legalistic in the way we relate to one another. We display the cross in conspicuous places as a symbol of our faith, but we seldom implement it in our daily transactions. We want our version of the truth to have priority, and yet we are confused about what we believe.

The truth we have most likely failed to grasp is

that the gospel is more than an ideal or a dream; it is an assignment. We must do more than exalt a story. We must apply its power. The gospel is first and foremost an assignment in love. We must love God as we love no other and we must love one another as we love ourselves. "Love" is a word which best describes God and it is an attitude which He requires from us. How can we love Him whom we have not seen if we do not love those we see every day?

The gospel is also an assignment in righteousness. It calls for a commitment to the highest ethical and moral behavior. It is not a false piety to which the gospel invites our attention. Jesus made it clear that our righteousness must exceed the religious display of the scribes and Pharisees. The gospel of righteousness emphasizes integrity as the basis of our belief and practice. Although our goodness is flawed by our sinful inclinations, honesty keeps us close to Him whose righteousness is sufficient. Our Christian pilgrimage is one which keeps us struggling to do that which is right in the sight of God.

Furthermore, the gospel is an assignment in faith. We walk where we do not see. We trust our Lord to lead us into the unknown. "Faith" is an action word. It motivates us to give sacrificially, to serve diligently, to talk gently, to live peacefully, and leave the rest to God. Faith allows us to be optimistic about life here and in the hereafter.

May we never take the gospel casually. Let us see it as our marching orders, our daily creed, our present hope, and our eternal reward.

- FIFTEEN -
IN PURSUIT OF GOD'S WAY

There is an awkward interpretation of the will of God which is confusing and illogical. It is the tendency to assume that whatever happens is God's intention. It's a simplistic approach to life which reads into every event God's specific plan. It is a subtle way of blaming God for all of life's transactions. For folk who want quick, easy answers to life's complexities, this may be sufficient. For those who need a redemptive word in the midst of crises, this view of God's will is devastating.

The problem with this interpretation is that it does not differentiate between what God permits and what God intends. It tends to ignore the freedom which God allows in an evil world. The truth of the matter is that God does not cause, nor does He approve, all of life's sinful and destructive episodes. He is not the author of confusion, nor does He design our downfalls.

Of course, most of us believe this; but in our rush to find a simple solution to some crisis, we misrepresent God. It is difficult to find comfort from the One we hold responsible for our grief. In our haste to defend His sovereignty, we end up giving God a bad reputation. Our weakness is that we must always have an explanation. To describe something as being "the will of God" becomes a catch-all cliche for that which we really do not understand.

Sometimes we may be more accurate to admit we do not know rather than to resolve our ignorance in some kind of fancy "God-talk." We'd best be careful what we claim for God, lest we use His name in vain. Often it is nothing more than spiritual pride when we feel compelled to have an answer to every complicated question of life.

Our pilgrimage with God is mysterious and profound. It requires a commitment of faith and prayer. The truth which sets us free and calms our spiritual anxieties is not lazy truth. It is worked out in the struggles of our souls. In thinking God's kind of thoughts, we grow in His grace and knowledge. In so doing, we are comforted by the integrity of our search to know the perfect will of God.

- SIXTEEN -
COMMITMENT ENERGIZES

In many ways our commitment to God can minimize the most pressing anxieties of our lives. Our deepest frustrations are often the result of an improper allegiance to the things which really matter. There is a godly dimension to life which adds stability to our thinking as well as our actions. Our most satisfying moments are those in which we synchronize our wills with His. Commitment to God is the ability to relax in the way He has put our lives together. Because we are pleased with His ultimate design for all things, we participate in His dream for a better world.

To receive Jesus Christ as our Savior means that we are prepared to make a significant investment in His Lordship. He creates within us a need to reach out redemptively toward others. In expressing His kind of compassion, we find relief from the annoying bitterness and resentments of life.

In practicing our Lord's approach to those who sin against us, we lose the compulsive need to retaliate. The love which the Lord places within us tends to calm the angry billows of our souls. We no longer need to hate, even if we feel it is for a worthy cause. The confining grip of greed is dealt a devastating blow when we honor the mandates of Biblical stewardship. The faith which emerges from our relationship with

God is an avenue toward peace as we face the disconcerting aspects of life.

In true belief we walk with God, trusting Him not so much for an easy road, but for a journey that has infinite possibilities for good. Yes, there are many ways in which commitment ministers to the emotional, spiritual and mental needs of our lives. The extent to which we allow God to provide our priorities is the degree to which we can find a happy and meaningful life.

- SEVENTEEN -
LIFE'S DEEPER VALUE

One of the amazing things about life is the close relationship between the spiritual and the material. It is as though the sacred and the secular are one. The tangible derives its worth from the intangible. Our possessions as well as the events of our lives have no real value apart from our state of mind.

If there is no spiritual content to the way we live then what we have and what we do has little meaning. Sometimes we talk about "mind over matter." In reality what we have on our minds is what really matters. It dictates our ability to enjoy the material aspects of our being. In no way can we exclude the spiritual ramifications of life's events.

We may take a vacation, but unless our souls are prepared for such an event there is little rest and relaxation. Emotional baggage is much more stressful than arms full of luggage. Family reunion cannot be a happy event if there are strained relationships. We can never find satisfaction and fulfillment in our work if there is tension with co-workers. A beautiful house can never be a home without love and forgiveness. Fine cars are nothing but transportation unless there is faith for the journey. Technology may give us relief from tedious chores. It may add hours of free time to our lives, but only God can add peace to our pastime as He becomes Lord of our leisure. Friends are nothing but acquaintances until there is a bonding of souls. Church is only a building unless there is genuine commitment to the things of God.

The bottom line to all this is we cannot enjoy life if there is inner strife. Guilt, resentment, retaliation, jealousy, unforgiving hate, and the likes will destroy all of life's parties. The joy of whatever we do, wherever we go, and however we live comes from the condition of our hearts. The abundant life is one in which the spiritual is in harmony with the physical. The invisible ministers to the visible. We enjoy life, not because we are perfect, but because we struggle toward it. Repentance and faith are our best tools in working out our own salvation. In fact, there is no salvation nor happiness apart from them. Be happy inside where it really counts.

- EIGHTEEN -
GRACIOUS LIVING

Gratitude is an attitude that comes from the deepest recesses of our soul. It is not something we try to manufacture. It is the way we approach life. In many ways gratitude reveals the condition of our inner being. Our thought processes are conditioned by whatever thankfulness we feel. Our speech reflects the degree to which we are grateful. Even if we try to express a pretended thanks we come across as being insincere. Whatever joy we have in life is a product of our thankful hearts. Whatever peace we experience comes from a gracious inner contentment. Happiness comes when, from the core of our being, we can express thanks.

Grateful people are those who do not become disgruntled with life's strange turn of events. They do not presume that life owes them more than they are getting. There is a sense of acceptance about things over which they have no control. There is a commitment to correct the things within their power to change.

Grateful people live out of the resources of faith. They trust the eternal goodness of God, believing that righteousness has the power to survive. Grateful people are responsible stewards of life's blessings. They feel an obligation to invest in the recovery of the less fortunate and in the healing of a sick society. Prosperity and prominence do not weaken the witness of thankful people. They are equipped to praise God from whom all blessings flow.

There is an interesting correlation between grace and gratitude. Gracious people recognize their undeserving status. They humbly receive the love of God and freely share His love with others. Without gratitude grace would be taken for granted. There would be no deep appreciation of God's sacrificial event. There would be no evangelistic fervor and no zeal for ministry.

May the Lord God of heaven and earth energize our capacity for thanks-living as well as thanksgiving. May the words from our lips, the meditations of our hearts, and the deeds of our hands express glorious thanks to our generous God.

- NINETEEN -
SPIRIT-LED CONCLUSIONS

One of our problems with honest Biblical interpretation is that we want our Bible to specifically address every issue. We want it to give simple, pat answers to all our complicated questions. When it does not, we twist and bend certain passages to give us our desired result. We manipulate the Word of God to suit our own interpretation.

The truth is, the Bible does not explicitly supply us with easy solutions to all our problems. For this reason it is dishonest to make certain passages say things never intended. The Bible is God's inspired Word on many issues and it gives us direction and guidelines for all issues, but a specific conclusion on so many matters is ours to discover.

In no way does this minimize the authority of Holy Scripture. In reality it allows the Bible to point to something greater. If the Bible had told us everything, there would have been no need for the Holy Spirit. Jesus told the disciples before His departure that He had much more to tell them, but they were not ready to grasp it. He announced the coming of the Holy Spirit who would lead them into all truth. Here, then, is our clue for approaching today's complex issues. We must seek the guidance of the Holy Spirit. Our Lord has not left us without a leader.

Of course, a question arises. How do we know our understanding is of the Spirit? For one thing, it will be consistent with the scriptures. It will reflect the spirit of Jesus as He dealt with the issues of His day. There will be no malice or jealousy in the way we discuss our opinion. We will be open to what others have to say on the matter. We will be firm in where we search for truth, but not dogmatic in our decisions. We will leave room for the Holy Spirit to correct our mistakes and redirect our thoughts.

A closed mind on any issue cannot enjoy the fruit of the Spirit. We are not sufficient within ourselves to have all the answers. We do not own the scriptures and neither do we own the Holy Spirit. We must allow them the freedom to speak to us whenever and however they choose.

There is a wonderful peace in permitting the Holy Spirit to control our lives, even our interpretation of scripture. Love is a marvelous tool for learning.

- TWENTY -
HOLY BIBLE, BOOK DIVINE

It is important for Christian folk, who place so much validity on the Bible, to understand why it is such a vital book. In fact, our deeper appreciation of the scriptures rises in relation to our understanding of the kind of book it is. Once we grasp the enormous magnitude of this God-breathed revelation we can never minimize its word for our lives. We call it the Word of God for indeed it clarifies His nature and makes known His will. No other literature gives us a historical as well as a devotional perspective on the things of God. The Bible shows us the interaction of God in human affairs and we see it as salvation history. The music of its message draws us to God in a sense of worship and praise. The Bible is the tangible source to which we turn for divine instruction and inspiration.

Of course, it does not give us answers to all the issues of life. It does give us, however, a mental attitude and a spiritual disposition with which to approach life's complexities. The Bible teaches us to be honest about our ignorance and humble about our knowledge. Because we do not know everything, we stand in the shadow of this great body of truth and allow its all-encompassing presence to dictate the direction of our thoughts and behavior. We study it not for the purpose of angry argumentation but sincere edification. We lose its sense of grace when we approach the Bible as though we have the only interpretation. God is much bigger than any thoughts we may compose about Him.

At best, our Biblical interpretations are limited, and for this reason we must draw from the insights and opinions of others. In the formation of our scriptural convictions, we need the Holy Spirit to give us a teachable and tolerant mentality. We must not try to own this Word of God lest it becomes an idol which we control and manipulate. We finger lovingly the pages of holy writ, not for the purpose of worshiping it, but that we let its breathtaking inspiration carry us into the presence of God. When this occurs, the meanness in our methods of interpretation is lost in the love of God who has given us His word. People become more important than projects as we sing in one accord, "Holy Bible, book divine, precious treasure, thou art mine." The Bible becomes the word of God in our hearts and we celebrate its unifying power.

- TWENTY-ONE -
A CHARGE TO PERSEVERE

The Christian life is composed of people who keep on "keeping on." Saints are simply sinners who keep on trying. "Perseverance" is a mighty word in the Christian vocabulary. The powers and principalities of evil have a variety of ways to break down our resistance. We will not survive spiritually if we succumb to Satanic despair. When sin occurs in our lives, the tempter would have us lose faith in our ability to repent and recover. He would shame us into believing we are hopelessly depraved. The end result is that we surrender to our sinful passions.

Yet, the gospel of grace reminds us that we are more than the sinful nature we often express. Sin does not have to have the last word in our lives. Jesus came that we might have another chance. He died to take away our sins. He arose that we might claim His victory. He is at the Father's side to intercede for us as we articulate our confessions and petitions. God has made a big investment in us so that we can be "more than conquerors through Him who loved us."

We must clearly understand that discouragement is the devil's tool. He would have us give in to our selfish inclinations and give up on any hope of spiritual recuperation. In fact, others may join the devil in making us feel inferior and unworthy. In order to build themselves up, some folk would use our weaknesses to accent their strengths. In the process, we are left unassisted in our struggle for righteousness by those who glory in themselves at our expense. We must never allow certain people to spiritually intimidate us because, in reality, we are all recovering sinners.

We begin our struggle toward God with the understanding that we do not deserve to pursue Him. Yet, in His grace, He invites and encourages us to seek Him with all our emotional and spiritual energy. He uses our weaknesses as an occasion to demonstrate His willingness to lift. When we fail, He calls our attention to a more excellent way. We never sin away our opportunity to make a fresh start. If we persist, God is faithful to reward our spiritual ambitions. We are beautifully encouraged by His promise that one day we may hear Him say, "Well done, thou good and faithful servant."

- TWENTY-TWO -
CALLED TO PARTICIPATE

In our desire to be faithful Christians we spend many hours in church. Sometimes we attend and it is mere ritual. We go through the motions of worship and Bible study with robot precision. Because of its routine we never seem to grasp the reality of what is being offered. Our need to be entertained and excited robs us of deeper thoughts and personal edification. We lose our sense of being involved.

At times we approach church attendance in the same way we go to the movies. At the movies we plop down with a soft drink and a bag of popcorn, expecting the screen to give us some soothing moments of entertainment. If it does not produce to our liking we are disappointed.

Church is different because we are called into a fellowship of participation. For it to have meaning we must share in what is happening. If we are disappointed, it is partly our fault because we have been given a lead role in the drama of church life. Whatever is lacking may be our own contribution. The truth is, "the more we give the more we receive." Of course, others must share equally if we are to have a vital church experience.

There is nothing boring or routine about what God has done for us in Christ. If there is monotony in church, it is a human factor. It stems from either disinterest or false expectations. To lose ourselves in the goals and ambitions of God makes church the most exciting aspect of our lives, however poorly it may perform at times.

There are occasions when our need to blame God for life's difficulties causes us to be bitter toward church and church people. Our anger toward God is translated into cries of "boring sermons," "poorly taught Bible lessons," "it is not like it used to be," and "no one has reached out to me." All the above may be true, but first we must determine how much we have contributed to it.

We must not give up on God because we experience a drought of spiritual zest. It too will pass away, and if we are faithful there will come a time when salvation's joy will return. Songs will sound as if we wrote them. Sermons will be like letters mailed to our spiritual address. Bible study will be autographed by God with our name in bold print. Old things will have passed away and all things will become new. Monotony will give rise to spontaneity. Joy will replace depression and God will be alive in our lives. This does not mean the valley will never return; but when it does, we can anticipate another journey to the mountain.

- TWENTY-THREE -
DREAMS THAT OUTLAST LIFE

Former seminary professor John Carlton once said, "We are all going to die with half of our music still in us." How often have we seen someone struck down in the prime of life with many a song unsung, many a poem unwritten, many a chore undone, and many achievements yet to make? Even if we live to old age, the melody of our lives is still playing with many chords untouched.

The point here is there is a sense of unfulfillment about life. There is a craving in most of us to be as productive as possible for as long as we live. Of course, we will never completely fulfill all our ambitions. We will never reach our maximum potential in a hundred lifetimes. We are created with much more capacity than the proverbial fourscore years and ten can produce. Our dreams will always outlast our life.

For this reason there is a strong case for heaven. Surely heaven is a place where we go on living in the light of our highest earthly aspirations. Whatever God inspired us to think and to do on earth will have a heaven in which to find ultimate fulfillment. Our faith will not allow us to assume that our love, sacrifice, devotion, and grace perish in the grave. Shakespeare's Brutus was wrong. Good is not all-interred in our bones. The Bible's hopes that "we shall know as we are known" and "we will serve Him there" give an eternal dimension to the way we live.

Jesus said, "I go to prepare a place for you." We have every reason to believe it will be a "Jesus" kind of place. It will reflect the quality of His love, the character of His commitment, and the power of life itself. Whatever music is left in us will burst forth in a crescendo of praise to the almighty God and His saving Son. Whatever skills were left unperfected will reach a height of unimagined excellence. Whatever worthy dreams were left unrealized will have eternity in which to become reality.

No, it has not entered our minds what heaven is like. Yet it seems reasonable to assume God has put a little heaven-thinking in our minds so we can keep hoping, growing, and moving in heaven's direction. Even our speculation on the subject can have some moments of God-breathed insight. Sometimes mortal thoughts must give rise to the immortal and the corruptible must give rise to the incorruptible.

Let us, therefore, sing the songs of earth until life runs out here, and then we will join the chorus of heaven and complete our music.

- TWENTY-FOUR -
ANGUISH DISPELLED

"Master, had you been here my brother would not have died. I know that he will live again in the resurrection. I believe that you offer life in the hereafter, but now I need my brother. Death is so final in this life. It has taken away the one on whom I had depended.

"Lord, if you had hurried you could have gotten here in time. You could have been here before he expired and healed him. Why did you tarry, Lord? Did you not sense the urgency of the situation? You've been in our house many times, and my brother was one you loved. You should have hurried. You should have come when we called. We thought surely when you found out who it was, you would have come immediately. You could have kept him from dying. But now he is gone. We are without our precious brother."

Jesus said, "I am the resurrection and the life. He who believes in me will live, even though he dies; and whoever lives and believes in me will never die. Do you believe this?"

"Yes, Lord, I believe, but my brother has been dead four days. Even if you thought about healing him, now he is beyond hope. Death has the advantage, and the grave clings to its prey. Would even God dare to reverse a process with so many shocking implications?

"Yes, Lord, we will take you to our brother's tomb. We have many friends there now. Everyone loved him, and they are finding it difficult to believe he is gone. Lord, are you crying too? I know you loved him and he loved you as well.

"No, Lord, we must not remove the stone. I'm not sure I could take the sight of it. I would rather remember my brother as he was. I know you loved him and would like to see him, but it will not be a pretty sight. Let's just leave and go back home for a meal. Yes, Master, for you we will remove the stone, but please do not expect us to go in."

When the stone was moved, Jesus called in a loud voice, "Lazarus, come out!" and he did. "Take off the grave clothes and let him go."

Life cannot wear the garments of death.

- TWENTY-FIVE -
POSITIVE PRAYER

Prayer is an awesome aspect of divine fellowship. In fact, it is the heart and soul of our relationship with God. Although we communicate with our heavenly Father through Bible study, meditation, songs, and worship, it is prayer that defines and undergirds each of these. Perhaps the greatest privilege of our Christian pilgrimage is prayer. How blessed we are to be invited by God Himself to sup with Him and He with us. The availability of God to our sometimes awkward and inconsistent faith staggers the imagination. Prayer is our access to the heavenly Father through His Son Jesus Christ. Without it, God becomes a distant deity with no invited input into our daily circumstances.

Prayer is the most personal and private part of our relationship with God. For this reason, no one can ever keep us from praying. It cannot be legislated either in or out of our lives. We can offer our private prayers anywhere and anytime we wish. It is a matter of desire and need to talk to God. Our personal conversation with God need not interfere with anyone else's religious freedom. God deals with each of us as though we were the only one with whom He converses.

Jesus made quite a case for private prayer as He elevated the prayer closet over the street corner as a better place to pray. Of course, Jesus did not eliminate public prayer as a part of our conversation with God. On several occasions He offered beautiful prayers that He apparently wanted others to hear.

Jesus did know, however, that public prayer could get twisted and distorted because of improper motives. Praying done to impress others with either words or piety did not receive high marks from our Lord. Prayer requests that are made primarily to spread malicious gossip do not serve a compassionate purpose. Matters that would embarrass and discredit are better left for the privacy of the prayer closet. Prayer chains are not designed to be hotlines to the latest rumors, but sources of intercession for the latest needs which can be discreetly announced. Prayers that intimidate and subtly boast of our own goodness fit our Lord's definition of hypocrisy. Care must be taken that the public aspect of our praying is not weakened by ulterior motives.

Prayer, when used for its intended purpose, is nothing short of a miracle. To think we can talk to God about anything, anywhere, and anytime is super...no, it is supernatural. This does not mean our petitions will always be granted as we desire, but we are heard, loved, and given what God deems best.

Prayer does not always change reality, but it changes us to adjust to reality. Therefore, pray lovingly without ceasing.

- PART TWO -
PEOPLE POWER

"The Lord gives strength to his people; the Lord blesses his people with peace."
Psalm 29:11 (NIV)

- TWENTY-SIX -
PEOPLE POWER

The power of people to affect us is an interesting phenomenon. We are influenced daily by what people say or do to us. Sometimes it is what they do not say or do not do to us that makes a big difference in our lives.

We give other folk a big amount of control over the way we think and act. Our dispositions are often the result of our reactions to the way people have treated us. Our moods are made either better or worse depending on who has been messing with our minds. For some reason we seem to be programmed to let others determine if we are to be happy or sad.

We are incurably addicted to what others think about us. We give away our freedom to be our own person in hopes that we can be liked by other persons. It can be an awkward way to live if we are intimidated continually by the power of people and never find our real identity.

The strong influence of other people, however, does not need to be a negative factor in our lives. We can be motivated and challenged to do our best because they expect it of us. We can get a better picture of who we are from those who love us enough to share their honest opinions.

A certain amount of praise and congratulations are essential to our good self-image. We need others to encourage us on the journey of life. We must have the reinforcements of people lest we lose ourselves in a pool of self-pity. We need teachers, mentors, critics, spouses, family, and a supporting cast of folk to keep us on course.

We do not have to give away our identity, but we can give away our pride. Before significant others we can be humble without being humiliated. We can lean on others without losing our self-respect. The laughter of others can lift our spirits. Even the scorn of others can challenge our stamina. We can indeed be indebted to others.

Since we are surrounded by a multiplicity of people, the Lord God of everyone wants us to find our place. We are not lost in the crowd. We are energized by His grace and inspired by His people. We look down on no one and no one looks down on us because we are called to be sons and daughters of the living God. In the spirit of true servanthood we find all the reasons we need to love ourselves and to be loved by others, even as God loves us all.

- TWENTY-SEVEN -
SINNERS ANONYMOUS

An area of life in which most of us are skillful is the ability to sin. Our capacity to break the rules is an instinct with which we were born. Nothing seems to come more natural than our tendency to err. With little encouragement and no training at all we can sin with the best of the sinners. If such were needed we could all become consultants in the art of iniquity. Of course, no one needs tutoring to be more disobedient. Hopefully our struggle is to overcome our sinful ways rather than cultivate our personal evil.

If the conquest of our sin is indeed our goal then we might use our individual weaknesses to help one another. Perhaps we have learned some things about our besetting sins that we could share with others. Our private struggles help us look into the dark and devious ways of iniquity. The pain of our guilt equips us to warn others of sin's pitfalls. Yes, we *can* become consultants to one another--not in the art of sinning, but in the practice of not sinning.

Might it be that a person who struggles with lying could teach us the dynamics of dishonesty from an inside perspective? Perhaps the person whose weakness is to harbor hate has learned some ways to avoid its terrible tentacles. Surely a person who battles lust and greed has found some secret to lessen its selfish power. No one knows the horror of any sin like the person who struggles with it. Perfection is not required. We instruct as we struggle.

If we had the courage not only to confess our sins but to share the lessons we have learned in the battle, we could have a redemptive influence on one another. The fear of embarrassment, rejection, and gossip keeps our weaknesses within us. The subject of sin is too sensitive for most of us to discuss in an atmosphere where love and acceptance is not present. It would be great, however, if in some way we could take lessons learned from all our accumulated iniquities and apply them as a united front against the problem of evil.

Perhaps we could manage the force of temptation better if we found a fellowship of honest sinners with whom we no longer needed to pretend. We could work on overcoming our sins rather than laboring to disguise and deny them. Could it be that this is part of what church was intended to be? Since we are all at times overtaken by sin, we need to draw on one another's strength.

- TWENTY-EIGHT -
PEOPLE ADJUSTMENTS

Do you feel good about the people who are included on your list of acquaintances? Life has a way of exposing us to a variety of folk. Most of the time, we have little choice of those with whom we share life. We did not choose our parents and although we can choose a spouse, we cannot choose our natural-born children. We have only minor choices in classmates, working associates, and those with whom we share church.

Sometimes it becomes quite a challenge learning to adjust to folk in our lives who are there not entirely of our choosing. To some it may seem unfair to have been thrust into a pool of people whom we did not invite into our lives. For better or for worse, however, we have our lists of acquaintances. The interesting thing is that we can add to, but we cannot take away from, this list of folk who have crossed our paths in some obvious way.

The other side of this thought is that we are on their lists also. They did not choose us any more than we chose them. Who knows, they may be rebelling against the process that brought us into their acquaintance. We must not assume everyone who knows us is going to like us any more than we like everyone we know.

As we reflect upon this fact of life, we see the value of our Lord's lesson on doing unto others as we would have them do unto us. If we require kindness and courtesy from those with whom we share a bit of life, then we should express the same toward them. One of the greatest hindrances to good human relationships is that we expect more from others than we are willing to give. On the other hand, sometimes we give more than is required and become frustrated when others do not reciprocate.

It is a happy person indeed who can learn to accept and adjust to everyone on his or her list of acquaintances. No, we do not have to become "bosom buddies" with everyone we know, but we are required to treat one another with respect. It is a law of harmonious living to be tenderhearted and forgiving to one another, as God in Christ has been to us.

- TWENTY-NINE -
DISFRANCHISE

The word "disfranchise" means to take away certain rights and privileges. It is to be cut off from some of life's events. Sometimes this can be a legal act, but most often it is a subtle penalty we impose on people who are different.

There are a host of people living on the periphery of life simply because they do not conform to the majority norm. They look different, think different, dress different, and perhaps smell different. For any number of reasons certain people are cut off and separated from that significant entity to which they want to belong. They are left out of a part of life in which they wish to be involved. It is a cruel way society has of treating folk who march to the beat of a different drummer.

It can happen in church when a certain creed becomes more important than people. When a pattern of thought and a theological position take precedence over a kind disposition toward others, disfranchisement occurs. Church people who are so sure of their own righteousness can cut off those who they feel do not measure up. People who are considered spiritually inferior can feel disfranchised from those who enjoy flexing their religious muscles. There is a lot of rejection in church by people who ought to be the most accepting people in the world. It is sad when some folk do not feel free to participate in church because it seems to be for others. The tone of fellowship appears to be more exclusive than inclusive.

Home can be another source of disfranchisement. It occurs when material priorities become more important than family togetherness. Certain members get cut off in their search for emotional security. Their identity is lost in the struggle to maintain the family name and prestige. No one is more lonely than a family member who has everything and yet has no one. It is painful being kin to folk who do not cultivate kinship.

Young people are often victims of disfranchisement. Special little groups and cliques are formed to exclude so that insecure youth may have an identity. Those cut off are hurt by this subtle rejection. Somehow children learn early about "herd" mentality, but what pain it creates for the strays! Young people left on the sidelines with no opportunity to be on the team develop deep emotional scars. Disfranchisement is a painful penalty for being different, especially if you are young.

God's Word says, "Be ye kind one to another." Might we say, "Do not disfranchise one another by the way we talk or by the way we organize our friends." After all, life's franchise belongs to God, and He says, "Whosoever will, let him come."

- THIRTY -
WHO IS NEIGHBOR?

It was a hard saying when Jesus insisted that we love our neighbor as ourselves. We are not sure we want to share ourselves that extensively with anyone. Jesus further complicated the matter with His broad definition of neighbor. In fact, He exempted no one from being neighbor who had need of our attention and our resources.

Our human desire is for a rule that would release us from our responsibility for certain folk. We want to know how far away a person should be before he or she is no longer considered a neighbor. If geography is the criterion, then perhaps down the street and around the corner is far enough to be neighbor-free. If distance is defined in terms of belief, then perhaps those with different ideas, strange customs, or no belief at all can be excluded from our required list of neighbors. If race and politics and social circumstances can create a legitimate distance, then perhaps a lot of "undesirables" can be treated as non-neighbors. If poverty is our plight, we may excuse ourselves from being neighbor to the more affluent.

In whatever way we may wish to define and/or distance ourselves from our neighbor, we cannot ignore our Lord's simple formula. To Jesus, neighbor had nothing to do with geography, or creed, or race, or any set of circumstances. It was a matter of being at a place and at a time when our resources and our compassion were adequate to meet someone's need. No one has to qualify to be our neighbor. At its best, being a neighbor is a lot like grace. We reach into the depth of our being and find a reason to reach out to the best of our ability.

No one teaches us to be neighbor. It is a part of who we are in Christ Jesus. Our commitment to Him causes us to empathize with hurting humanity. His Holy Spirit causes our hearts to break by the things that break the heart of God. We grow to have a mind in us which is the mind of Christ toward the needs of others.

From this perspective, we do not necessarily choose our neighbors. Circumstances plunge us into the arena of life where those with whom we share life cultivate our opportunities to be neighbor. Some folk are our neighbors because they fit certain criteria for closeness. In a more Biblical sense, however, others are our neighbors because of their great need of us in a given situation. The neighborhood is the world and yet our neighborliness is as focused as our next occasion to meet a need.

- THIRTY-ONE -
NOUNS VS. ADJECTIVES

In grammar class we learn that adjectives modify nouns and pronouns. They are "helping" words used in describing places, persons, events, or things. Most of the time we put more emphasis on adjectives than we do on nouns. This is especially true in our treatment of people. We tend to place people in categories according to our description of them. Often we see adjectives rather than people. "Red" and "yellow," "black" and "white" are adjectives. "Republican" and "Democratic," "southern" and "yankee" are adjectives. "Conservative" and "liberal," "fundamentalist" and "atheistic" are adjectives. "Educated" and "ignorant," "cultured" and "uncouth" are adjectives.

The nouns are "mankind" and "womankind." The pronoun is "us." Somewhere along the journey we must discover the nouns or else we will destroy ourselves over adjectives. It is so easy to get caught up in the ways of describing people that we never really see people. Prejudice is the result of our exaggerated emphasis on adjectives.

In our world of amazing diversity there are any number of ways to categorize people and things. The context in which we were reared conditions us to form our philosophy of life. The way we look at things and people determines the adjectives we use. In our reservoir of words we can choose to use good or bad adjectives. We can allow these helping words to give us a positive way of describing people and things, or we can use our adjectives in a negative context.

No one was freer of letting adjectives determine His outlook on life than Jesus. He taught us to look into the hearts of people and evaluate them for who they are rather than what they are called. He did not come to die just for those with pleasant adjectives. He died for all people, regardless of their category. He established an all-inclusive fellowship called "church." The best way to describe the people of His kingdom is "Biblical persons." The words indelibly written on every human being are "Made in the image of God." Our Maker has made it clear that no one is inferior who bears the resemblance of the Heavenly Father.

Sin creates any number of adjectives which separate us from one another. Our personal iniquities define us in ways which make us less desirable. Because we have all sinned, our greatest need is to struggle toward being a "Biblical person." When this occurs, such words as "kind," "forgiving," "trusting," "loving," "serving," and other Biblical adjectives will best describe us. We will also focus on nouns and pronouns instead of adjectives.

- THIRTY-TWO -
CHALLENGE OF THE ENEMY

How do we deal with our enemies? Now that is a tough one, is it not? Of course, the normal reaction is that we dislike them. We discredit them and hurt them for hurting us. We tend to build ourselves up as we tear them down in hopes of conquering by our superior sense of importance. We divert attention from ourselves by questioning the spirituality and integrity of our enemies. Usually we prefer the more subtle methods of innuendoes and half-truths to keep our hatred from being so obvious. We would rather camouflage our deeper hostilities in an effort to conceal the sinners that we are.

None of this helps, however, because we know that it is not the Christian way to deal with our enemies. No matter how we try to disguise our hate, it has a way of rearing its ugly head to hurt us more than anyone else.

It is important, therefore, that we learn to appropriate the spirit of Christ in dealing with our enemies. Somehow forgiveness, love, and grace must converge upon us to keep us from returning evil for evil. Somewhere we must gain the courage to stop the cycle of hate by receiving the last blow and initiating reconciliation. There is nothing more beautiful in all the world than eliminating our enemies by making them our friends. Of course the question arises, What about those who refuse to be our friends? Some people will reject us no matter how hard we seek a right spirit.

The constructive thought here is that we can learn from our enemies and even grow in Christ as we absorb their hostility. Our enemies can keep us humble and dependent on Christ in a way our friends could never do. Opponents keep us alert to the fact that we are human and sinful and that our discrepancies are offensive to others. If it were not for those who dislike us we might never consider our personality weaknesses. Perhaps God can use our enemies more than our friends in our struggle with repentance and faith.

In the spirit of Christ our enemies will never really defeat us unless we give them that power. If our enemies refuse to treat us kindly, then let us make opposition our friend as we learn all God teaches through adversity. Our opponents can help keep us close to the cross where we will hear a familiar voice saying, "Father, forgive them, for they know not what they do." Here is where we can truly pray for those who despitefully use us and turn the other cheek as we forgive in the power of Christ.

Let us make friends with God's children and, as much as lies within us, live peacefully with all people.

- THIRTY-THREE -
INADEQUATE JUDGMENTS

For many of us, perception is reality. What we perceive a thing to be is what it is in our minds. Usually our first impression forms our final opinion of people and circumstances. We seldom give ourselves the benefit of another point of view or a reassessment of our original perception.

We tend to judge people on the basis of our first information about them. If our first encounter is unpleasant we have difficulty forming a better opinion. If a friend gives us bad words on a person we quickly allow that to influence our total impression. If we see something that has the appearance of evil we are prone to jump to awkward conclusions. It is so easy to misinterpret what we think we heard in relation to what was actually said. How quickly we judge someone prematurely with limited facts.

Perception can be a fickle feature of our opinion-forming process. In many ways it is at the mercy of our sinful, selfish nature. We tend to see and hear what we want to see and hear. Our ability to have a positive outlook on life is inhibited by a faulty perception. Jesus said if our eyes are evil then our whole body is full of darkness. If the way we look at things is always conditioned by a negative disposition, we will never develop a God's-eye view of any situation. The only way we can come to proper conclusions and have a healthy perception is to allow the light of truth and not the darkness of half-truth to influence our opinions.

A willingness to forgive and a commitment to grace are our greatest allies in forming a proper perception. Everything will look bad if we want it to look bad. No amount of apology will solicit our forgiveness if we are not conditioned by grace. To see most people in a better light we have to shower grace upon them. It takes a lot of the grace of God to improve our perception of things.

Only in Christ can we see beyond what people and circumstances seem to be to what they are and what they can be. Although we must guard against becoming gullible and naive we can rethink our first impressions. Grace requires us to take a second look while honesty improves our faulty perceptions. May God help us in our struggle to overcome hasty conclusions.

- THIRTY-FOUR -
COLORING OUTSIDE THE LINES

The phrase "coloring outside the lines" refers to the actions and disposition of folk who do not always function within the confines of that which is generally accepted. These folk are not inhibited by majority opinion. They are not controlled by what everyone else wishes them to think and do. They have a mind of their own.

For the most part, these are the people who give us new inventions. They challenge the way things have always been, offering us new ways of facing old problems. Creativity abounds when there is a willingness to color outside the lines. Sometimes the unusual and the unexpected can shock us out of the way things have always been to the way they can be better. As a society we are indebted to individuals and groups who have had the courage to challenge the status quo by offering a more hopeful and helpful way.

On the other hand, coloring outside the lines can be disastrous. Changing everything does not necessarily represent a better way. People who are different just for the sake of being different are not always different for the right reasons. Some folk who color outside the lines are obnoxious and difficult, while others are vain and vulgar. There are some things which are tried and true for the centuries. Our world has some absolutes from which we deviate at our own peril. We do not experiment with moral and ethical behavior. We cannot produce a better society by total replacement. We build upon sound structures by changing only that which has served its effectiveness or that which tends to demoralize and destroy. It is wrong to treat an ingrown toenail by amputating the leg.

In many ways Jesus colored outside the lines. He colored outside the lines in terms of outmoded religious customs. He dealt differently with sinners, Samaritans, women, and other folk of lesser standing. Jesus colored outside the lines when it came to such things as love, forgiveness, prayer, worship, sacrifice, and grace. He was not a conventional Rabbi nor was He an acceptable prophet in most people's eyes. Yet, He did not come to destroy the law or the prophets but to fulfill them.

Let us, therefore, be courageous enough to "color outside the lines" when the issues are right versus wrong. Let us not color outside the lines, however, just to be obnoxious and difficult.

- THIRTY-FIVE -
LOVE CLOSE UP

It is often said, "to know them is to love them." The idea behind this statement is that when we are close enough to know other people's motives and inner ambitions, we can appreciate them for who they are.

It is true that our dislike of some people occurs because we have a misconception of who they are. We have allowed the opinion of others as well as misinformation to create a false appraisal. How often have we had to change our impressions of people after we really got to know them? We discovered virtues and dreams much more worthy than we had previously assumed. The truth of the matter is that most people have some good points which, at a distance, we never give ourselves an opportunity to explore. In fact, we keep some people at a distance because we think we do not want to know them close up.

It must be a part of our human frailty to need a few folk to dislike. What could we talk about with our friends if we could not spend some time discussing our enemies? After all, what are friends for if they will not support our personal prejudices? Perhaps a true friend is one who will help us discover the better side of our enemy. Nothing is more soothing to our sensitive souls than the knowledge that someone is not as bad as we had imagined.

Of course, the flip side of this is that some people look better at a distance than they do close up. Getting to know some folk close up reveals idiosyncrasies not obvious in casual contact. Here again, distance creates an unrealistic expectation which causes us to place certain people on pedestals. We set ourselves up for disappointment when we exempt them from being human, too. For some reason, it demoralizes us to discover our heroes have clay feet. It is a subtle kind of idolatry in which we long for someone with all the answers.

We are in trouble, however, when we expect this of anyone other than Jesus. Our best human relationships come when we can know other persons, warts and all, yet love and respect them for who they are. We learn to forgive discrepancies in others as we develop wholesome, realistic friendships. When we can accept people for who they are, then "to know them is to love them."

- THIRTY-SIX -
THE CROSS OF FRIENDSHIP

Friendship is a fragile item on life's agenda. It demands a lot of attention to prevent breakage. There is so much to misunderstand and so many wrong ways to interpret actions and words. Friendship can give us much pleasure, but it can also cause much pain.

There is a sense in which we make ourselves vulnerable to everyone we consider a friend. Friendship requires us to give a bit of ourselves away. Sometimes the giving is not reciprocated. Mutual investment of time and energy is what makes some people friends while others are only casual acquaintances. Yet, people who keep score are often disappointed when their expectations are not fulfilled. A truth to remember is that we can have only so many "best friends." Sometimes we overload ourselves with more "best friends" than we have time and energy to maintain.

Jealousy and envy can create tension for struggling friendships. Friends who compete for attention, accomplishments, and accumulation of things often become weary of the relationship. When greed is a goal it is hard to meet the sacrificial demands of friendship.

Nothing damages our ability to relate to others more than an attitude which is haughty and proud. We all tend to gravitate to people who are humble and kind. We enjoy being around folk with whom we can be ourselves. Having to pretend and exaggerate our importance is not a comfortable setting for friendship. Friendship thrives when we can celebrate each other's good fortune.

Another enemy of friendship is disloyalty. Nothing is more painful than the knowledge that someone has shared our confidences. It hurts when people gush over us in public and stab us in the back in private. We seldom recover a friendship where disloyalty prevails. How beautiful are the people we can count on to be our friends through life's stormy details!

Jesus gave us a great principle for friendship when He said of Himself, "Greater love has no man than this, that he lay down his life for a friend." The truth here is that in every serious friendship we lay down some of our life. We give up something for the good of another. We deny ourselves and take up the personal cross of friendship as we follow our Lord's admonition to lose our lives in order to find them. It might be said another way. We lose ourselves for another in order to find someone who will do the same for us. He or she who would have friends must accept the sacrificial demands of friendship.

- THIRTY-SEVEN -
MOTIVATION BY GUILT

There is no good reason why we do it, but we all do it in subtle and devious ways. We put one another on guilt trips, trying to get each other to do and to be what we desire. Perhaps we all live with excessive guilt and seek to hammer others into submission with a similar pain. Our greatest ally in manipulating other people's lives is their weary conscience. When made to feel bad enough, most of us will do anything to buy a good feeling about ourselves. Our poor self-image makes us vulnerable to those who would use it to their advantage.

One of our greatest sources of unhappiness is our inability to distinguish between bad guilt and good guilt. Bad guilt keeps us forever in someone's debt. Our need to please keeps us in the throes of anyone who seeks to manipulate our minds and control our activity. Bad guilt produces emotional stress and serves only to disturb and destroy.

Good guilt, on the other hand, has a redemptive nature. It encourages repentance and right relationships. Its pain has a healing dimension as it becomes a deterrent to lingering hostility. It seems to be the nature of true Christian fellowship to use the energy of good guilt to create an awareness of God.

How sad when religion becomes a tool to badger

folk into some kind of emotional submission. How doubly sad when the Bible is used as a club to coerce the spiritually naive. Surely church was designed to be a place where guilt is dissolved by grace, and a poor self-image is lost in an atmosphere of restoring love. Would it not be great if in church we heard only words of encouragement instead of pious phrases of a guilt-provoking nature? If only we could learn to help one another with our guilt, church would truly become a redemptive fellowship. Friendships would be more lasting and family life would be more satisfying.

It seems like such a simple thing, but we disrupt relationships daily because we want to make people pay for their misdeeds and awkward words. For some strange reason, we want others to know that we know they are bad or wrong. What a different world it would be if we all were kind to one another, tenderhearted, forgiving one another as God in Christ Jesus has forgiven us.

- THIRTY-EIGHT -
TOUGH LOVE

Tough love is a way of describing affections that seek to be responsible. It is a love that struggles to be authentic. Tough love requires a sense of accountability in every relationship. It is not permissive and condescending. It does not say and do things simply to flatter. It does not love for the sake of getting, but for giving.

Tough love is concerned for what is in the best interest of those it loves. It does not thrive on popularity but on perseverance. It has a wholesome interest in what is right rather than what is expedient. It does not try to please everyone at the expense of anyone.

Tough love will weather the storm of many disagreements. It will find ways to express respect without violating convictions. It takes a stand for what seems right and does not acquiesce to a stronger voice that seeks to manipulate.

Family love is a tough love. It requires a lot of give-and-take to allow home life to be healthy. Dysfunctional families are often lacking in tough love. Sometimes parents equate love with permissiveness. Children resent tough love as being too harsh. Husbands and wives who have tender egos refuse to follow the principles of tough love when difficult times occur. Family living is not always easy. It can survive, however, when love gets tough with whatever threatens its happiness.

Leadership love is a tough love. It offers opinions and guidance based on what is good for the larger constituency rather than a favored few. Leadership love makes the unpopular decision knowing it will be uncomfortable. It suffers in silence with criticism and misunderstanding. Leadership love has the courage to challenge that which would be divisive and detrimental to its constituencies.

Christian love is a tough love. It is patient and kind when circumstances are harsh and hateful. It does not keep score. It does not measure love expecting the same in return for what was given. Christian love celebrates that which is good and adjusts to that which is bad. Its greatest reward is to see hate and fear give way to love. Christian love is a saving love, and saving love is tough. As it did for our Lord, it involves a cross. It gives itself away, bearing upon its innocence the guilt of others.

Tough love is life's most potent force. Go ye therefore and love one another.

- THIRTY-NINE -
SECRETS FOR KEEPING

Secrets often come in a variety of packages. Some secrets are designed to surprise. Certain facts are concealed in order to startle a recipient of a gift. Battle plans are hidden from the enemy to launch a surprise attack. The element of surprise is always dependent on secrecy. Another set of secrets is designed to protect our privacy. What is everybody's business is nobody's business. Because we live in a world where unscrupulous folk would take advantage of us, we cannot go public with our financial affairs. Secrets about our private fears and idiosyncrasies protect us from embarrassing comments by insensitive people.

We withhold certain personal information because there is a private aspect to our being. We have a personal relationship with ourselves containing things only God needs to know. Because we are private as well as public creatures we will always have secrets.

Secrets, however, have a way of seeping through our most sophisticated concealment. For one thing, certain people are always prying into who we are. They make it a point to investigate and analyze everything we do and say. They pose as friends, but in reality they are searching for the cracks in our armor. Once they find them our secrets are exposed.

In another sense there are people with whom we

think we can confide. We bear our souls to such friends with many of our well-kept secrets. That person then bears "our soul" to someone else considered confidential, and before long our private life is the topic of public discussion. When this occurs we have a tendency to withdraw and bear our souls to no one. We turn inward wondering if there is anyone we can trust.

At best secrets are fragile. We do not live in a confidential world. Sinful folk are always looking for someone weaker than themselves. Gossip is a thrilling pastime for people who enjoy sharing our secrets or anyone's secrets, for that matter.

How, then, do we protect our secrets? In one way it would be well not to have some secrets. Sin can cause secrets. Unresolved guilt makes us cling to them. Perhaps we protect our own secrets of human frailty by protecting others with similar secrets. "Judge not that you be not judged" is applicable because "we have all sinned and come short of the glory of God." Confidential people will most likely be treated confidentially. We tend to reap the seeds of gossip that we sow.

- FORTY -
LISTENING EARS

Communication is one of life's most necessary events. The ability to convey our thoughts to another person and to receive their thoughts as well is indeed a blessing. Words, whether written or spoken, become the vehicle by which we express what is on our minds.

Words beautifully arranged in perfect composition or in eloquent speech, however, do not necessarily mean communication has occurred. We may write or say what we really mean, but unless the one reading or listening is on the same frequency we may not accurately communicate. Words sometimes fail us because of the human tendency to misunderstand. How frustrating when our best attempts to communicate are misinterpreted. Good communication occurs when we work hard at giving and receiving the same signals.

It is not always other people's fault when they misunderstand what we think is clear speech. We may need to sit where they sit and listen with their ears to what we are saying. Seeking to understand another's misunderstanding is one of life's most loving expressions. We all have an emotional as well as a mental vocabulary. Some words have an emotional meaning which is not found in the dictionary. The cultural and psychological circumstances which birthed us have a lot to do with what we hear and what we say. To grasp this reality is an aid to good communication.

Sometimes we hear only what we want to hear. Our thought processes are so slanted we find it difficult to be objective in our listening. When this happens it is easy to quote someone out of context. We express the opinion of others from the perspective of our own opinion. Such mishandling of another's conversation greatly hinders communication. It gives the appearance of dishonesty even though we simply repeat what we thought we heard.

Jesus understood the human defects of speech and hearing. On one occasion He said, "Let your 'yea' be 'yea' and your 'nay' be 'nay.'" In other words, say what you mean and mean what you say. He also said, "He that hath ears to hear, let him hear." Jesus asks us to listen with discernment and integrity.

When we speak and listen in love, good communication will often be the end result. May the words of our mouths and the listening of our ears be acceptable in His sight.

- FORTY-ONE -
POWER OF OPINION

One of the great adjustments in life is the fact that we share our little bit of earthly space with a lot of other folk. For the most part, we do not live to ourselves but in relationship to others. This has the potential for being both a blessing and a curse.

It is a blessing when we are privileged to have people around us who care for us at the deepest level of our being. We do well to cultivate relationships with those who are inclined to be friendly. Everyone needs to surround himself or herself with a circle of friends who add to, rather than take away from, one's self-respect. It is to our advantage to share life with folk we find compatible.

The journey of life is too short to spend more time dealing with adversaries than cultivating friends. Surely it is God's design that we live peaceably with all people. Yet human frailty can cause an erosion of our best relationships. For this reason, we have to adjust to the fact that those with whom we share life sometimes can be a curse. Most likely, we all are surrounded by at least a few people who think they know more about us than we know ourselves. The tendency to be analyzed and scrutinized on a daily basis eventually takes its toll on our otherwise gentle disposition. Someone has said that never in human history have so many people known exactly what is wrong with everyone else. We live in a world of opinionated people and somehow we must come to terms with what others think about us.

A negative opinion about us does not need to be demoralizing. After all, it is the conclusion of someone who has very limited information. The most important opinion there is about us is the one we have of ourselves. Our ability to live with others will never be any better than our ability to live with ourselves. Critical words may hurt, but they will never defeat us if our self-esteem is secure. "Sticks and stones may break our bones, but words can never hurt us" if we truly seek the mind of Christ in dealing with the opinions of others.

Let us, therefore, praise God for people who offer us a variety of challenges as well as the opportunity to love and be loved.

- FORTY-TWO -
BREAK BREAD TOGETHER

Have you ever given much thought to the spiritual value of family meals? It's not that the table becomes a place for confession, condemnation, and parental sermons. In fact, if such should occur with exaggerated frequency, digestion would most likely be disturbed. Meals should not be mixed with trying to fix whatever is wrong with certain family members. Confrontation and argumentation can create a variety of heart burns.

The family meal is a time to enjoy food with those we love. In the relaxed atmosphere of family togetherness, the act of eating has spiritual as well as nutritional value. Whether God is mentioned at all other than at the blessing is not the issue. Theology and religion are not the only topics for wholesome family table talk. When there is respect and a healthy flow of conversation on any worthy subject, a meal can be as powerful as any form of public worship. Perhaps there is no other family activity that has as much potential for nourishing our bodies, minds, and souls as does eating together. Daily bread that is planned for and prayed about makes the kitchen a sacred altar and the dining room a sanctuary.

If this sounds a bit too symbolic for our secular ears, then note the importance of eating in the scriptures. In the Old Testament, every religious ceremony of any consequence was celebrated with some kind of feast. The gospels highlight eating activities of Jesus which culminated in the Last Supper. Coming together for common meals was a practice of the early church.

We must conclude, then, that eating involves more than physical survival. It is a ritual which has magnificent possibilities for fellowship and love. Eating together can impact the family in a positive way. Yet a recent survey reveals that, according to those questioned, over seventy-five percent of American families eat less than ten meals together in a week. Thirty-seven percent interviewed did not eat any evening meals together.

Although there are some legitimate reasons for these statistics, nonetheless, the family is robbed of an important gathering time. It's like a church having a flurry of valuable activities but never pausing to worship together. Mealtime gives a family a reason to gather in the midst of so much which causes them to scatter. A family who eats together in love will be doubly nourished for life's responsibilities.

- FORTY-THREE -
IMPACT CHRISTIANS

In professional sports, sometimes a person is referred to as an "impact" player. This means that the presence of that person's skills has a tremendous effect upon the team. It can often change them from losers to winners.

In a sense, Jesus is calling all of us to be impact persons. He wants us to make a difference as Christians in our world. He equips and encourages us to be people of grace. The energy of divine love is our contribution to the team.

The exciting truth which confronts us is that each of us can make a difference. The victorious possibilities of our personalities are limited only by our fears and lack of faith. The significance of who we are in Christ is enough to positively impact those places and people in life wherein we invest ourselves. The contribution which, by God's help, we are capable of making has mind-boggling implications for the kingdom of God.

There is no reason for any of us to fret over the fact that we are "undergifted." God, in His wisdom, has given us gifts suited to His design for us and according to our willingness to be used. There is no such thing as a loser in the economy of God if "we do the best we can with what we have for Jesus' sake today." Nothing is more stimulating to our spiritual ambition than to know that God has no one else just like us. Each of us is the very best He has in our category.

There is no way to escape our roles as impact Christians. God is counting on us to turn the franchise around as His church marches triumphantly onward. In His love, He projects a time when "every knee shall bow and every tongue confess that He is Lord of all." But until that time, He is expecting us to help "His kingdom come and His will be done on earth, as it is in heaven."

Jesus took a handful of folk getting nowhere with their lives and turned them into a band of disciples. They became impact players as the New Testament records their penetrating influence on that pagan world.

Our Lord continues to call quite ordinary folk like us to make a difference. Whether our sphere of influence is small or large, we are equipped to make a redemptive impact upon our social and spiritual environment. It's God's way of making winners out of losers.

- FORTY-FOUR -
"FAMILINESS"

In the beginning God created into the dynamics of human existence a sense of family. There is a need deep within each of us to relate to a mother, a father, perhaps brothers and sisters, as well as kin of all kinds. No one is an entity unto himself or herself. We belong to a natural family which gives us identity, tradition, and a perspective on life.

Our blood kin provide us with a family tree which, for the most part, we can be proud. In ancient days it was important to protect the family name and to keep the bloodline going. Even today we feel protective and caring toward those who share our name. When being introduced to someone with our last name we immediately begin pursuing the possibility of being related. Although we may sometimes rebel against our natural family and take our prodigal journey, we can never escape its effect upon us.

There are families of folk other than our natural ones to whom we may relate. Our church family can be composed of folk who are as close or closer than our blood relatives. In Christ Jesus we are called to be brothers and sisters within the fellowship of church.

There is also a family of folk with whom we work. Sharing several hours of the day pursuing common goals can create an occupational bond.

Working conditions are greatly enhanced when there is a sense of fellow-workmanship.

There is likewise a family of folk we call our circle of friends. These are people with whom we share common interests, common loyalties, and common adventures. They sometimes become more "family" than family. Friends are people who add a positive dimension to our lives. We are energized by their presence and encouraged by their conversation. Friends offset the negative spirit of our enemies. They sustain us when others seek to subvert us.

Furthermore, there is a family of folk with whom we may not share church, nor work, nor close friendship, yet they have an interest in our well-being. This family provides our medical care, fixes our car, serves our food, collects our garbage, repairs our roof, runs our government, and performs a multitude of duties to improve our quality of life.

In many ways we are blessed by a sense of family. God the heavenly Father is surely pleased when He observes His children seeking to be family to one another. The human family as the apex of God's creation has ways of expressing its "familiness" not yet explored. God grant us the wisdom and the will to be family.

- FORTY-FIVE -
CHURCH-WORTHY TRUST

When church is really being church, it functions on the highest level of trust. There is no way a fellowship of love can be established without it. Trust is the ability to believe in, to lean on, and to accept the contribution of others as vital to our own spiritual well-being. Trust is the product of humility and inner honesty. In trust we confess our own inadequacies and seek to find in others as well as God the completion of ourselves.

In church we deny our tendency to be in charge as we submit to the authority of grace and a godly disposition. Church at its best does not have a dictator nor a clique nor leaders with selfish agendas. Because of trust, the leadership of the church becomes a servanthood. People are trusted to do their best and are given the freedom in Christ to develop their own spiritual personalities. No one has to become the religious clone of some super-Christian. Leaders are trusted also to do their best without imposing upon them an unreasonable expectation. Christian leaders are called of God to expedite His agenda. In doing so, trusting God and trusting others are essential for any achievement.

Of course, we make ourselves vulnerable when we trust. Human frailties and inconsistencies will often produce disappointments. In church, where we lean so heavily on one another, we can be hurt.

A truth to be discovered, however, is that only God will never let us down. If our trust is sufficiently grounded in Him, our trust in others will survive the pain of betrayal. After all, why does the Bible say so much about forgiveness and love and restoration if we are not expected to renew our trust in one another? Church cannot be church unless there is a willingness to trust those who at times even struggle with their own trustworthiness.

- FORTY-SIX -
BACK TO THE FUTURE

Someone has said, "The future is not what it used to be." Here is a fertile thought whose author is unknown. Perhaps we could speculate as to the disposition of the person who would make such a comment. Maybe it was a pessimist who had a dismal attitude toward the future. It may reflect someone's inability to express hope. In this person's mind the negative may dominate the positive, always creating a bleak outlook. He or she may have become so disillusioned with life there is little for which to look forward. It is an unsettling way to live, but many are afflicted with strong doubts about the prospects of a better world. They tend to feel the best is behind them and the future can never be what it used to be.

On the other hand, however, the comment may have come from an optimist. The statement could express great hope in the future. This person may sense that the greatest days are ahead. In his or her eyes the future may be brighter than it has ever been. In this person's mind the positive always prevails over the negative, creating a sense of hopeful anticipation. If the future is not what it used to be, it could be better. The past may have given the present a reason to believe that life can improve in the future. It is a beautiful way to live and has the backing of the scriptures which point to an end time of joy and celebration. It is a matter of faith that we trust the processes of life to lead us to God's special future.

It may be possible that the statement was made by an older person who is trying to adjust to change. The kinds of things he or she anticipated early in life are no longer a reality. The years have taken their toll and the future looks different through aging eyes. It's not a matter of the future being better or worse. It is simply different. Changing times give an older perspective a new vision. The future is not what it used to be because nothing is what it used to be.

Furthermore, the statement could have been made by a young person. It may be that young eyes do not see a future as bright as their predecessors'. Youth have a way of questioning and challenging a system they feel has jeopardized their future. They also have a capacity to dream the impossible dream. They have time and health on their side. For them the future can be what they make it.

Whether optimist or pessimist, young or old, the words of a gospel song may speak best to us about the future. "Many things about tomorrow, I don't seem to understand, but I know Who holds the future, and I know Who holds my hand."

- FORTY-SEVEN -
SEARCHERS AND LEARNERS

The first people who came to Jesus were searchers. They were looking for something to fill the God-shaped void in their lives. They found in Jesus not only a word from God, but the reality of God Himself.

Once they were convinced of His Messiahship they became learners. They listened to His teachings and drew inspiration from His object lessons. They were open-minded people who were not locked into a prescribed way of thinking and acting. They did not require their Messiah to echo their own religious prejudices. In contrast to those who rejected Jesus, His followers were free to let the winds of a fresh spirituality blow upon their minds. They were free to participate in a love that reached in all directions toward all kinds of people. Forgiveness was no longer merely seven times at best, but "seventy times seven," or unlimited. The other cheek could be turned without appearing weak. Investing oneself for the good of others became a lifestyle rather than a reason to complain.

These and other great concepts of our Lord became the impetus for those first folk to follow Jesus. Of course their commitment to Jesus was not a total departure from their religious upbringing. It was not

Jesus' intention to destroy the old, but to build upon it and to fulfill it. He wanted to expand the concept of Messiah to include a God's-eye view of the world. Traditional Judaism had tended to focus on the externals of their faith. He wanted them to see beyond the law, the prophets, and the formalities of their religion.

Jesus accented fellowship with the Father as the focal point of faith. The temple with all its religious paraphernalia was nothing if it became a substitute for a personal relationship with God. Jesus respected the temple and all for which it stood. He was often in the temple area teaching, healing, and pointing people to God. He could not, however, tolerate the misuse of a place designed by God for godly purposes.

Here, then, are our simple lessons. Discipleship today is still a matter of being open to the freedom of the Spirit. We are still searchers and learners of the truths Jesus taught. We must never allow the vehicles of our faith to become the objects of our faith. Only God is God and nothing He has given can ever be a substitute for Him.

- FORTY-EIGHT -
COOPERATIVE FELLOWSHIP

Church at its best is more than a spectator experience. It is a fellowship of people equipping themselves for ministry and witness. The call of God has always been for His people to be actively involved in making a redemptive difference in the world. Church, therefore, is a learning resource, a training ground, and an experimental laboratory for the art of Christian living. Whatever transpires in the context of church is of great importance to every area of our lives. We cannot attend church in the same way we go to the theater. An entertainment mentality is not conducive to discipleship.

Church at its best requires a commitment to the higher things of life. There is no call like the call of God, which finds expression in the church. It challenges the moral and ethical fibers of our being. It pleads with us to minimize the things of the world as we maximize spiritual realities. Earthly ambitions are flavored with Godly motives. Love of self is defined only in the context of love for neighbor and love for God. Wealth is seen against a background of need. Stewardship becomes a matter of properly using that which we have. Ministry becomes the password of our lives as compassion grants us entrance into the hurting side of society. If we are serious about God we cannot leave church in the same way we leave the theater. A take-it-or-leave-it attitude does not produce commitment.

Church at its best is a fellowship of Jesus followers. We do not go it alone. There is a body of believers to whom we relate. In the strength of togetherness we struggle with the issues of life. God calls us into spiritual cooperation where we honor Him by honoring one another.

There is a public dimension to our faith. Lest we become spiritual hermits, we sing some of our songs and pray some of our prayers with our brothers and sisters in Christ. Church gives us a place to observe and experience the operations of grace. The power of people energizes us to seek the will of God and in so doing find a reason for which to live.

Church at its best is our most wholesome inspiration to do our best because "the church's one foundation is Jesus Christ her Lord."

- FORTY-NINE -
HOLY WAR

Isn't it strange that through the centuries men have gone to war and cut one another's throats, strongly motivated by the fact that they could not agree on what was to become of them once their throats were cut?

The power of religion to provoke hostilities and incite the atrocities of war is a fact well-documented in human history. We would like to think that religious motivation for war was unique to primitive people and that today we are more redemptive in the expression of our faith.

The truth is that on careful scrutiny of recent wars, they have all had their religious implications. It seems that among the basic hatreds of humankind are dislike and distrust of those who have a religious orientation different from ours. We tend to be terribly suspicious of people who have a different form of worship and call God by another name. Of course we have love in our religion, but most often it is only a love for our kind.

We are prone to project a lot of hostilities in the name of Jesus. There is a lot of anger in our religious pronouncements as we verbally chastise those who do not conform to our understanding of God. We would gladly call down the wrath of God on folk who spurn our kind of spirituality. How easily our compassion for the "heathen" turns to passion for their destruction.

There will always be wars and rumors of war as long as competing ideals of the world are allowed to clash. Jesus said, "He who lives by the sword shall die by the sword." There is a "sword" mentality in each of us which must be conquered by our Lord's sacrificial love.

"Turning the other cheek" and "going the second mile" may be God's word for all who are prone to fight in the name of Jesus. Our Lord's peaceful spirit will not allow us to go to war on His behalf. Our egos and our need to defend our pride of thought always cause dissention.

Let us hear His words again and again: "Peace I leave with you, my peace I give to you; not as the world gives, but my peace." In Him there is really no need to fight about what happens to us once our throats are cut.

- FIFTY -
GOD AND GOVERNMENT

The success of any nation is no greater than the patriotic commitment of its citizens. The accumulated power of people for law and order creates a civilized mentality. When majority opinion rules out divisive and subversive elements, a country can function as a united people.

"One nation under God" gives our nation a rallying point. Not that we all have the same concept of God, but together we recognize a power bigger than our own legislative bodies. Our search for God in relation to government enables us to dream for whatever divine reasons we have to exist as a nation. Although correctly we must separate church and state, we must not separate religion and government. Perhaps we *cannot* separate the two. We bring to the processes of government of the people, by the people, and for the people all the influences of our faith.

Belief in a supreme being, however we express it, gives us a strong appreciation for that which is above and beyond our frail attempts to govern ourselves. If we can understand and accept the greater government of the universe, then we can implement its principles into the lesser government of humankind. Without some grasp of God we lose the inspiration for the political process.

From the Christian perspective we are encouraged to pray for our leaders and strive to be law-abiding citizens. Jesus taught us to render to our government the things which government requires and to render to God the things which God requires. God and government are not the same, but they require a similar commitment. If we are obedient servants of God we will be loyal citizens. We will stand for the things which make our nation strong.

Religion in America is like a patchwork quilt. Each piece must be sewn together to make a proper covering. Without betraying our own convictions we must hold hands with people of other persuasions if we are ever to be "one nation under God." It seems that the nations of the world who are most cruel and unjust are those who seek to impose a radical belief system upon their citizens. Religion has a terrible capacity to become intolerant. When it has the power of government to force its rigidity, people become puppets of the state. Conformity is the goal of such countries while freedom of thought is severely punished.

Perhaps our most patriotic prayer in America is one of thanks. We express gratitude for our land of the free and home of the brave. Of course we pledge our allegiance to the flag and stand for our national anthem. In a profound sense, however, we pledge our allegiance to God and we sing, "Standing on the promises of God, our Savior."

- PART THREE -
PERSONAL VOLTAGE

"The Lord is my strength and my song; he has become my salvation."
Psalm 118:14 (NIV)

- FIFTY-ONE -
PEACE WITH OUR PAST

Making peace with our past is essential to our spiritual health. On our journey through life we accumulate a lot of emotional baggage. The past tends to leave us with an assortment of mistakes, mistreatments, and missed opportunities. The accumulation of guilt, resentment, and fear can become a burden too heavy to carry at times.

We come from imperfect backgrounds which have contributed to our own personal perplexities. Most of us have a lot to live up to and a lot to live down. Whatever our past has been we have to adjust to its realities. We cannot pretend it never existed. Our past is just as real as the present. Our inner child of the past is still with us. Yesterday's ledger affects today's balance sheet. We cannot fully escape where we have been, what we have done, and who has shared a part of our pilgrimage. Our past is like a boomerang. We cannot completely throw it away. It keeps coming back to influence our daily decisions and to affect our peace of mind.

In making peace with our past, honesty is our greatest ally. The ability to look back with integrity has many healthy implications. Because memory can play tricks on us, we can read more into a past occurrence than the truth can support. Memory can be exaggerated or minimized, whichever serves us best at the moment. As best we can, we need to let the past be the past and treat it with truth and grace. The pain of looking back occurs when there is an unwillingness to forgive and forget. In making peace with the past, not only do we forgive others but we forgive ourselves. We learn to let bygones be bygones as we move redemptively through the present into the future.

Whenever we make peace with our past, it will be a spiritual experience. Faith is a prerequisite, repentance is a necessity, and grace makes it happen. The truth of the matter is that in Christ we can experience peace about our past. Dysfunctional relationships can be healed in the light of His forgiving love. Mistreatment, rejection, and lifelong anxieties can be resolved when we are serious about making peace with our past.

Perhaps Paul said it best when he wrote, "But one thing I do, forgetting what is behind and straining toward what is ahead, I press on toward the goal to win the prize for which God has called me heavenward in Christ Jesus." Having peace with our past is indeed a work of grace.

- FIFTY-TWO -
WHO AM I?

One of the amazing discoveries about ourselves is how much "what we do" is related to "who we are." Often when others think of us it is in terms of our special skills or occupation. The value of our personhood is often set by the quality of our workmanship. People have a tendency to evaluate us in terms of our working performance. To a great extent, our self-image is built around what we do and how well we do it. This has both a positive and a negative connotation.

On the positive side, it develops within us an ambition to do our best. We take pride in our assigned task as we cultivate a healthy work ethic. We sense the value of paying our own way and pulling our own load. We develop a caring attitude in the way we relate our work to the progress of society. We grow to feel good about ourselves when we can see the call of God in our daily chores.

On the negative side, however, there is a danger in finding our total self-esteem only in what we do. If our worth is measured only by our work, what value do we have when we no longer can work? There must be more to us than a job description. We will soon outlive our usefulness if production is the only word that defines us. There is a deeper meaning to "who we are" than "what we do." We derive our worth from a creator God who looked upon what He had made and called it good. We thank Him for the creativity of our minds and the productivity of our hands, but we also praise Him for instilling His image within us. We are equipped to receive His Holy Spirit, to think His thoughts after Him, and to have fellowship with our heavenly Father.

We must not ignore these God-given attributes in the development of our self-understanding. What we do and how well we do it are certainly important to our self-image. Yet, who we are, Whose we are, and how we got to where we are must be given strong consideration. To be known only by what we do is a limited definition of our total personhood. Becoming a workaholic does not excuse us from experiencing the deeper things of life.

God help us to be able to lay down our work and rest in the knowledge that we have other sources of worth. We will have no peace or rest until we are willing to let God be God instead of making work our god. As we labor for the Master we find self-worth in being as well as in doing.

- FIFTY-THREE -
MOTIVE SEARCH

Motive is a strange, yet significant energy within our lives. It is the power of our personality. It is the driving force of our ambition. It is the reason why we do what we do, say what we say, and are who we are.

Nothing moves us like our motives. It is important, therefore, to understand our motives if we are to understand ourselves. This is not always easy because often our motives are subtly camouflaged so that we do not honestly know why we do what we do, say what we say, and are who we are. Sometimes our motives are clear and pure, while at other times they are fuzzy and ulterior. The fact that we do religious things does not always mean we have high religious motives.

Jesus, who looks deep within us, once observed that everyone who says "Lord, Lord" will not enter the kingdom of heaven. He often verbally chastised scribes and Pharisees for making a spiritual appearance so as to attract human attention. The motive for prayer is best expressed in a closet where a desire for public praise does not distract. The motive for benevolence is always weak when excessive attention is called to the gift. Jesus cut through the rules and regulations of traditional religion and focused on the reality of God's revelation. He taught His disciples to examine their motives in the light of God's loving purpose and not their own self-interests.

The call to deny oneself is a demanding discipline. It is embarrassing and painful to discover how much of what we do, what we say, and who we are is a subtle promotion of our own ego. Our praise, our prayers, and our proclamation can easily become an occasion to call attention to ourselves. We cannot seem to escape the fact that we have a terrible need to be noticed. Yet we must not allow this need to keep us from serving the Lord. He who calmed the boisterous waves can subdue the selfish uprisings of our souls. He can use a strong ego for His glory. Our Lord can give us insight into our personalities which will produce a humble disposition. To know He loves us as we are inspires us to evaluate why we do what we do, say what we say, and are who we are.

No, our motives will never be entirely pure as long as we contend with our human limitations, but we do not have to surrender. Whatever drives us can drive us to seek godly goals and serve righteous purposes, however imperfect our vision may be. When Jesus said, "Blessed are the pure in heart," He was commending those who allow themselves to be motivated by a desire to please God.

Why, then, do we do what we do? Why do we say what we say? Why are we who we are? Our struggle with these questions will go a long way in purifying our motives.

- FIFTY-FOUR -
GROWING THROUGH RISK

Most of us spend much time and energy looking for a sure thing. We try to live our lives with as little risk as possible. It would be great if life came with a solid guarantee that nothing unpredictable would arise. What if any chance of ever losing our job was all removed? What if all our investments were guaranteed a maximum return? What if a school made certain every student could earn perfect grades? What if a marriage contract could be written to eliminate every element of risk? What if a church could assure its members all their needs would be met and all their questions resolved? What if God suddenly offered guaranteed results for all our efforts?

We could go on "what if-ing" for a long time, but life is not put together that way. The faith factor has to be considered in everything we do. Life is risky business. We take a chance every day we live. Faith is our greatest asset because it helps to relieve the tension of total risk. It causes us to see that God is love and all things work together for good if we love Him. Faith allows us to see beyond the immediate circumstances to future possibilities.

We do not stick our heads in the sand and ignore life's difficulties. We accept risk as a legitimate aspect of human life. At times we are hurt by it, yet we learn from it. It stimulates our fear, yet it cultivates our trust. God is never nearer than when we look up through the dark pit of our despair to see the bright light of His love.

As long as we live, risk will never be eliminated, but it can be creatively anticipated. By faith, we can live on the "tiptoe" of expectancy, where every new emergency is an adventure with God. This does not presume a life of "fairy tale-ism." Hard knocks will come and sometimes their blows will be difficult to absorb. The Chinese word for "crisis" has two characters. One means danger. The other means opportunity. Perhaps there is a lesson here. Risk may mean danger, but it can also be an opportunity to grow.

If risk overwhelms us we cannot live by faith. When this occurs we lose a sense of stewardship about life. We are reluctant to invest ourselves in anything worthwhile unless the returns are obvious. We cannot depart with our tithes and offerings lest our security be threatened. Fear settles in as we prefer a more predictable way of life. Our strength, however, comes from making peace with risk.

Life is always at some turning point. We must make sure the point around which it is turning is God.

- FIFTY-FIVE -
PERSONAL STRUGGLE

The greatest need most of us have is not to have things done for us but to find the motivation and resources to do things for ourselves. We are, to some extent, dehumanized when we cannot participate in our development, disappointments, and recoveries. While there may be times when we become either emotionally, mentally, spiritually, or physically dependent on others, we must not lose our ability to dream our own dreams and pursue our own goals.

God has created us and equipped us with the tools for our own existence. He is not going to do for us what we can do for ourselves. He wants us to struggle and grow through the circumstances of life. Even though at times God may appear to be cold and uncaring, He is cheering us on as we try to make the most of any bad situation. He understands the perplexities with which we deal. God knows the complexities of the issues which confront us daily.

As best we can understand God's disposition, it seems that He trusts us with decisions and their eventual results. He does not spoon-feed us with spiritual baby food but allows us to taste the bitter herbs of life. We are free to make our own mistakes, yet He encourages us to grow wiser through regret and recovery. Neither faith nor commitment immunizes us from whatever life might impose upon us. They equip us to draw on our own inner resources. We are energized by life's challenges, which pose the possibility for either success or failure.

The fact that we cannot know the eventual outcome of our decisions and circumstances keeps us close to the One who does. We pray for His direction and petition Him for wisdom. Even though we are basically on our own, we are not alone. God's presence prevails to inspire us toward right thinking and living.

The machinery of life comes with a good instruction manual. God's Word advises us for the journey. It illustrates the need for proper conduct as well as wholesome commitment to the things which really matter. While life's book does not come with all the answers in the back, it does encourage a disposition which longs to resolve difficulties.

We can make the most of any situation when God's will is our clearly defined motivation. Let us, therefore, thank God for His special input in our lives and take courage as we face whatever the future holds.

- FIFTY-SIX -
THE LIGHT WITHIN

Have you ever considered the ingredients of an ugly face or the makeup of a pretty one? Ugliness is not always the result of cosmetic blemishes nor is beauty the product of perfect skin. Both are reflections of inner attitudes that come from the core of our being. Some folk have a beautiful countenance even though their physical attributes are limited. Others are ugly even though they are beauty candidates. If "beauty is as beauty does," then "ugly is as ugly does." Our thoughts and our actions have far more to do with our attractiveness or lack of it than any physical qualities we may possess.

The ancient Hebrew writers used the heart as a symbol of one's inner thought processes. The psalmist cried, "Create in me a clean heart, O God." Proverbs tell us, "As a man thinketh in his heart, so is he," and, "A merry heart produces a cheerful countenance." Jeremiah explains that "the heart is deceitful above all things, and desperately wicked." Ezekiel reminds us that God can give us a new heart and a new spirit. Jesus said, "Blessed are the pure in heart." The writer of Hebrews summarized it all when he wrote, "It is a good thing that the heart be established with grace." Scripture makes a strong case for soul beauty, which is the first step in good grooming.

However we may look on the outside is largely determined by what we are on the inside. If one has a sour disposition it will most likely be revealed in facial expression. A negative, hateful attitude produces frowns, snarled lips, and ugly contortions. One does not complain and criticize with a beautiful smile. It takes an ugly face to express our deep-seated hostility. Hate has a way of taking its toll on eyes that without it would have a peaceful gaze and on cheeks that otherwise would be flush with a smile. Pride and greed give our faces a stern and determined look. Expressions of worry and fear create wrinkles that are unbecoming. Sorrow gives our face a sad look as despair is written boldly across our brow.

A happy heart, however, creates a pleasant countenance. Faith has a way of bringing out the smile in us. Our conversation with God adds a dimension of beauty to our facial features. The light within us cannot be hidden behind a frown. It bursts forth in the glow of a tranquil appearance.

So cheer up, my brother and sister, and live in the sunshine. Let the smile of God shine through you as your face reveals the joy within. Put on a happy face, because ugliness, as well as beauty, is somewhat contagious.

- FIFTY-SEVEN -
EGONOMICS

There is an interesting, yet unfamiliar, word that has made its way into a few people's vocabulary. The word is "egonomics." It combines the word "ego," which basically means "self," with the word "economics," which suggests management of one's material welfare. "Egonomics," therefore, is a study in how the "self" is ingrained in what we buy, where we go, and what we do with our material resources.

We live in an "I-deserve-it" generation. We buy things not so much because we need them, but because we owe it to ourselves to have them. We go in for designer things. We want our material possessions to reflect who we are. We make statements with our clothes, our hairstyles, our automobiles, our houses, our trips, and whatever we put on display. Nonconformity has become the new conformity. Being different helps our "self" to stand out. Hence we have "egonomics."

When we bring the concept of egonomics into the realm of religion we have an interesting phenomenon. We have folk looking for a designer church. Everyone wants his or her kind of worship. The need to be different is more important than the need for content. Style takes precedence over substance. The flashy and the exotic are "in," while the traditional or whatever has been is "out." We worship the new no matter how it may violate the old. No longer do we join churches for better or for worse. It is for better only. We have no commitment to better the worse. We move on to that which seems better for us. It is a consumer-friendly mentality which makes a church acceptable to the egonomic generation. Rather than denying oneself and taking up a cross, the tendency is to deny the cross, take up the self, and follow whatever is egonomically appealing.

Of course, there is nothing wrong with being different in terms of church. In fact, Jesus was rather creative when it came to religion. Perhaps He addressed this issue when He said, "I have not come to destroy the law and the prophets, but to fulfill them." He was not throwing the baby out with the bath water. He was merely proposing some new bath water.

The worship of self has been around a long time. Egonomics is not new. It's as old as sin.

- FIFTY-EIGHT -
TIME-WISE

Time is a fascinating feature of our human existence. It is the stuff life is made of. We may lose some important items of life, but time is the most precious thing we could ever squander. We may be rich in worldly goods, but poor indeed if we have no time.

Our sins are often complicated because of the lack of time. We do not have enough time to make all the money we crave. We do not have enough time to satisfy our ambitions. We do not have enough time to go all the places there are to go. We do not have enough time to make everyone our closest friend. We do not have enough time for all the available thrills and excitements in our world of entertainment. We are often trapped by our perceived lack of time and it raises our frustration level to the point of indigestion. In our attempt to do it all today we overload our daily human capacities. We try to borrow so much today from tomorrow that if we are not careful we will bankrupt our souls before our years are spent.

Life is passing us by far more quickly than we can absorb it. The longer we live the less likely we will live any longer. Yet, many of us go on living our lives as if there will never be a change of schedule. We become fanatically committed to a routine we

We become fanatically committed to a routine we assume will last forever. We have a work ethic that causes us to labor even during our leisure. Health and circumstances, however, have a way of inserting some unexpected holidays. Disease can play havoc when our bodies are fatigued. The fast lane takes its toll on our emotional and spiritual stability. Suddenly we find ourselves sidelined simply because we refused to take some time-outs.

Rest is not the only cure for our misuse of time. Worship can also heal our exhaustion. Taking time for God is taking time for ourselves. The Creator has a way of resuscitating His creatures. We are made to have fellowship with God, and to ignore it is to add spiritual fatigue to the weariness of our flesh. To see God in the daily flow of things has a calming effect on all we do. It enables us to make the most of our time because God does not make impossible demands of our time. He frees us to find fulfillment within the parameters of our daily allotment of time. As the songwriter suggests, "take time to be holy."

- FIFTY-NINE -
MAINTAINING COMMITMENT

Isn't it strange how quickly we can make commitments in relation to how long it takes to fulfill them? We say "I do" in a matter of seconds and yet it is a lifetime obligation. In a moment we sign for a house and then there are twenty-five years of payments. So it is with cars, children, business, and career commitments. Life has a way of holding us to our original agreements. We cannot violate our vows without some penalties. It is a brief transaction to join the church but then come many years of prayers, attendance, worship, giving, fellowship, witnessing, and all the joys and sorrows of being God's people. It takes a matter of seconds to receive Jesus as our Savior and Lord, but what do we do with the rest of our lives?

Conversion has a beginning but it has no end. Commitment to Jesus is never a finished product. Unlike our business transactions, we never make a final payment. The Christian life is a journey. Its destination has eternal dimensions and, for this reason, we never complete its requirements in this life. God is always beyond us and we keep pressing toward the goal.

It is a matter of faith that we cultivate our spiritual capabilities as we hunger for a relationship with God. Our reach must always exceed our grasp, or what is heaven for? God has created us with aspirations and dreams. We are made to long for that which is complete and perfect. We soon learn that this is a lifelong investment. Just as we do not own a house simply by signing the original contract, we do not become godly by a few periodic gestures of goodness.

We grow in the grace and knowledge of our Lord. It is a daily walk with Him that leads toward fulfillment. What we do with the rest of our life, after commitments have been made, is the stuff life is made of. It's a process of making the most of that which we know to do. We invest ourselves in the kinds of commitments we make. If our vows have value, our lives will be productive. If we waste our substance in riotous living, then we spend our years in the far country. Our need is to make worthy commitments and do the best we can to fulfill our dreams.

- SIXTY -
KNOW THYSELF

Self-evaluation is a process that goes on within us with daily regularity. It's not so much a checklist of items which gives us a reading on how we are doing. It is a subtle personal appraisal of everything we do and say. It is part of our self-image which monitors our standing with others as well as with God. Even though we are not always conscious of it the process goes on. We are constantly making judgments as to whether or not we are equal to given situations. Consciously or subconsciously, we evaluate our performance in every area of life, and as we do we need to avoid two extremes.

First, we must avoid being excessively lenient in our self-appraisals. It is easy to see ourselves as better than we really are. We must avoid becoming cocky and overconfident so that we overpower others with a sense of our own self-importance. Nothing weakens our witness as a Christian like an assumption of spiritual superiority. It is interesting how we can look on the faults and failures of others as serious character flaws and yet minimize our own discrepancies. Just because our sins are different does not ever mean they are any less evil in the sight of God. It behooves us to look at ourselves honestly and realistically.

On the other hand, we must avoid the extreme

of being too hard on ourselves. It is easy to think of our sins as worse than anyone else has ever committed. We look at other people and think they would never have our kind of thoughts or do our kind of sins. We assume we are some kind of sinful oddity, forgetting the Bible says "we have had no temptation to confront us, but such is common to man."

Never learning how to lay our sins on Jesus, we desperately try to carry the whole load. Perhaps this is why we like the gossip circuit. We find some sordid satisfaction in learning about others whose sins are as bad as ours. We long for someone we can look down on. We try to prop up our low self-esteem by running other people down. This does not lessen our load, but adds to our accumulating guilt. The devil always wins when we allow sin to give us a spiritual inferiority complex.

The truth of the matter is that our sins are no worse nor better than those of others. From God's perspective we gain no advantage nor disadvantage in comparing iniquities. No matter how evil and devious our transgression we have not sinned past our ability to call upon God. It may be from the pit of ugliness that we look up and live. In confession there is relief. In repentance there is hope. In Christ there is grace, which is our best resource in knowing how we are doing.

- SIXTY-ONE -
CROSS OR FEEDING TROUGH?

There is a cultic kind of condition developing within Christianity today composed of people who only want to be fed. They run from church to church, book to book, tape to tape, and to all types of media attractions trying to hear something more to their liking. For these folk, being "fed" usually means hearing something which confirms their opinions. It supports their point of view or, as is often said, "It meets my needs." For the most part it is an entertainment mentality with a religious appeal.

In many ways such persons have taken the cross out of their faith and replaced it with a feeding trough. They eat and eat, but they seldom burn any of their spiritual calories in real religious exercise. Often a negative disposition develops when the latest feeding fad loses its luster. The new food is no longer new and the new voice settles into a tedious monotony. Itching ears begin to search for a more satisfying word.

Perhaps the answer to this feeding frenzy is to take off the bib, put on a towel, and wash some feet. Push back from the table and go to work in the fields that are ripe for the harvest. Dress in the full armor of Christ and do some Christian soldiering. Our Lord who said, "Come sup with me," also said, "Go into all the world and make disciples." He who said, "Feed my sheep," also said, "Deny yourself, take up your cross, and follow me."

Of course, it is right and proper to desire spiritual food. Teaching and preaching are essential to our religious diet. Just as our physical growth is dependent on good food, so is our spiritual progress. It is essential that we expose ourselves to that which gives us a healthy understanding of God. Our minds are indeed a part of our religious commitment. The Bible commends those who thirst for the truth.

Hearing and learning, however, are not enough. James tells us that hearing the word of God and doing nothing about it is like a man looking in a mirror and then immediately forgetting what he looks like. There is more to the Christian life than finding a good feeding trough. It is discovering a place and a way of interacting with the needs of the world. It is a beautiful life when the need to know is complemented with the need to go.

- SIXTY-TWO -
PERSONAL HYPOCRISY

There is a strange and complicated reality with which we all must live. It is the inevitable hypocrite that dwells within us. Even though we hate to admit it and often try to conceal it, part of us is a fake. There is a considerable amount of emotional and spiritual cover-up in the way we live. There is a lot of "put-on" in the way we do things. Just as some women put on makeup to display smoother skin, most of us put on the kind of face expected of us. We put on a disposition that does not necessarily reflect our true inner feelings. We smile when inside we are crying. We laugh at things which are not humorous. We talk a different game than we play.

Because we are possessed with a need to please everyone, we strive to be politically correct in every situation. Our subtle insincerities become such a way of life that we tend to lose touch with who we are. In reality, we deceive ourselves as much as anyone else. The mask we wear hides the person we see in the mirror as well as the one we display to others. We have multiple disguises which can be used depending on the circumstance.

How do we deal with the hypocrisies which define us? Is there any way to relax the false face we feel compelled to wear? Authenticity is a worthy but difficult goal. Our greatest need is to discover and admit, at least to ourselves, the depth of our deception. To understand these personal discrepancies is to find the root cause for many of our iniquities. Most of our dishonesties are not because we choose to lie. We simply do not have the courage to tell the truth. The truth about who we think we are is too painful to reveal.

Only in Christ can we find enough acceptance and love to relieve our need to pretend. In Him and to Him we can confess our innermost secrets and get on with the kind of life He intends for us to live. God does not require us to be super-Christians. If He did He would not have invited us to repent. He must be embarrassed when we try to project a perfection we do not have. Surely our most authentic witness comes from our struggle to "be" rather than what we pretend to be. Whatever goodness we have is not ours. It is His. As the poet said, "Nothing in my hands I bring, simply to Thy cross I cling."

- SIXTY-THREE -
A PROPER ANGER

The energy of anger is a force to be reckoned with in our world. It can cause nation to rise against nation. It can cause neighbor to mistreat neighbor and families to crumble in pain. It can cause normally decent people to harbor hatred. It can cause all of us to lose our composure and make fools out of ourselves.

What is there about this mysterious power which causes us so much inner pain and frustration? Sometimes anger gains its strength from our exaggerated selfishness. It receives momentum from the "mighty me" complex. Anger preys on our weaknesses to make us feel strong. It makes us defensive and resentful toward those who detect the flaws in our armor. When we allow the sun to go down upon our wrath it complicates tomorrow's relationships.

Misdirected anger can be one of our most harmful emotions. Yet it does not always need to be bad. Paul said, "Be angry and sin not." Perhaps this is Paul's way of acknowledging a proper anger. It is a proper anger that runs money changers from the temple when it is obvious they are keeping others from worship. It is right to be angry about the hurts of life when they rise out of mistreatment and evil. Paul is telling us to channel the energy of wrath into constructive purposes.

As the Holy Spirit controls our lives, even the emotion of anger becomes a redemptive tool in the hands of God. As our anger is kindled against sin, we are energized to oppose it. There are things God does not want us to tolerate. He wants us to despise the sin that separates us from one another. He wants us to denounce the evils which destroy human personality.

Therefore, let us seek Him who can inspire us to be angry about sin and yet have love for the sinner. Let us be angry enough at sin to confess, repent, and turn from the awkward attitudes and actions which have stunted our spiritual growth. Let us be angry enough at hate to let love prevail, at fear to let courage inspire, at doubt to let faith direct, and at all uncleanliness so that righteousness might stand. Then and only then can we "be angry and sin not."

- SIXTY-FOUR -
LORD, MUST I GO?

"Go ye therefore into all the world," He said.

"Does He really mean that?" I thought. It is a big, cruel world out there. Rome does not deal kindly with new movements. Surely Judaism will not tolerate competition for her converts. Our half-pagan world does not understand a religion of love, grace, and purity.

"All the world" would mean telling Gentile folk about Jesus. I think we should keep His gospel for our Jewish people. After all, we are the chosen ones. He was birthed and nurtured by our kind. It was our scriptures that predicted His coming. It was our prophets who anticipated a Messiah. Why should we share this good news with anyone but our own? There are a lot of Gentile pigs out there who would trample the pearls of His marvelous story. Did not our fathers teach us that such people were unclean?

"All the world" could mean going to dangerous areas of foreign countries. It would be risky going to places where human life is cheap. Barbarians do not understand "turning the other cheek" and dying on a cross, crying "Father, forgive them." People could get killed trying to convince such pagans that God intended us to live with love instead of hate. The remote areas of our world are not advanced enough to grasp the meaning of God's Messiah. The only savior they know is whoever can help them conquer their enemies. Loving one's adversary and treating the enemy with kindness are not principles by which they wish to live.

"All the world" means going to those close to me who have thought my actions strange since Jesus came into my life. It means loving my neighbor as myself. What I know and have experienced with Jesus can be shared with my nearest critic and my best friend. Perhaps this is harder than going to the barbarians because these are people who know me, warts and all. I'm not sure I am good enough nor know enough to be effective in my own community. After all, Jesus said, "A prophet is not without honor except in his own town." There is a Samaritan family next door. How could I ever step foot in their house with the gospel? I did not even take food when their child died.

Surely He did not mean "all the world." My, my, that would include Gentile pigs, barbarian tribespeople, Samaritan half-breeds and the neighborhood riffraff. He must have meant it, however, because He whispered strongly into my ear, "Lo, I am with you always, even to the end of the age." I know Him well enough to know He would not send me somewhere without His companionship. I must confess. It is into "all the world" I have been challenged to go. Will you go with me?

- SIXTY-FIVE -
HISTORY LESSONS

If you had lived during the days of Noah would your lifestyle have qualified you for the cruise? Could God have used your kind of commitment to be the father or mother of a great nation as He did Abraham and Sarah? Would your ability to survive adversity have enabled you to pass Joseph's test? What kind of disposition do you think you would have had on the Exodus journey?

Had you lived in later Old Testament days would you have had David's love for God, Solomon's wisdom, Elijah's candor, Isaiah's insight, and Ezekiel's dreams? Could you have demonstrated the faith of New Testament disciples, the endurance of Paul, and the future hope of John? Do these and other spiritual heroes of the past give you reason for a more energized life in Christ? Perhaps these questions seem a little strange and yet they focus upon some essential components of our Christian faith.

One of the beautiful benefits of studying the Bible from a biographical perspective is that we learn from character association. We identify with ancient personalities. We sense their situation. We take their side and fight their fight. We join them in the faith. To mentally transpose ourselves to some circumstance in the distant past is to sharpen our ethical and moral skills for present situations. To observe as well as to understand ancient behavior gives us hope for our own spiritual survival. Although the leading characters in both Old and New Testament history had commendable qualities their frailties were also obvious. Sometimes we learn from their strengths, and again we learn from their weaknesses.

History is an awesome schoolmaster whose lesson assignments we must not ignore. Sometimes we do not learn because of our human tendency to believe the past will never repeat itself. We forget that life is composed of similar cycles for every generation. Although Biblical characters are cast in strange and primitive cultures, commitment or lack of it was the same for them as it is for us.

God seems to evaluate our faith response in the light of our particular advantages or disadvantages. Therefore, it seems that we who have a Bible full of personalities from whom to learn have a significant advantage. Ignorance of God's will can never be our excuse for spiritual failures. Yet somehow God knows we do not learn well and bids us look to Calvary as He whispers, "My grace is sufficient."

Whether we would have done as well or worse than Biblical people is not the issue. What we do now with Jesus the Christ is all that really matters.

- SIXTY-SIX -
THE MINISTRY OF HUMOR

Humor and laughter are a vital part of our human existence. There is a sense in which the funny things of life complement the serious things of life. The lighter side of living makes the darker side of living more bearable. To lose one's sense of humor is an emotional tragedy. The ability to laugh is a God-given outlet to reduce the sadness of our souls. When a smile bursts into laughter a lot of inner rage is released. The soul cleanses much of its negativism with good, positive humor.

There is close proximity between joy and laughter. In many ways happiness expresses itself with a sense of humor. People who can laugh at themselves and with others are often able to control the complexities of life.

Of course, it is important to laugh at the proper times and at the proper things. Laughter, like anything else, can become devious. Humor has a strange capacity to be unhealthy. When laughter is degrading, humiliating, and offensive it hurts rather than heals. When people are crushed by our humorous ridicule, we have violated the purpose of laughter.

Sometimes there is a lot of hostility in our humor. We joke of things about which we are angry. Our humorous sarcasms often reveal our hidden rage.

We jest with people and joke about circumstances rather than share our true feelings. Being comical can be a defense mechanism to hide our identity. The role of a clown meets our need for attention and acceptance. When we use humor for the wrong reasons, it adds a morbid dimension to our laughter. Some things about which we laugh are not funny in a healthy sense.

Yet, let us not despair of developing a good, healthy sense of humor. There is so much about life that lends itself to a humorous interpretation. There is a kind way for us to laugh at and with one another. Love can be revealed through our laughter as well as our tears.

There is indeed a ministry of humor which reaches deep into our lonely souls. It stimulates our joy muscles and makes our funny bones rejoice. It keeps us singing in the midst of despair and smiling when frowns might prevail. Because our God is a god of joy, let us never minimize the role of healthy humor in our search for happiness. Perhaps Paul said it best when he wrote, "Rejoice in the Lord always, and again I say, rejoice."

- SIXTY-SEVEN -
RELIEF FROM DESPAIR

Where do we turn when life tumbles in and there seems to be no light at the end of the tunnel? What resources are available when death stares us in the face pointing its bony finger? What happens when the underpinning of life begins to crumble and the house we thought would stand forever begins to lean? Who is our Savior when sin overtakes us with its horrible ability to enslave us? Where does faith come from when God seems to be on the other side of our problems? How do we keep on "keeping on" when "keeping on" leads us to a pointless frustration?

These are legitimate questions which flow from hearts that are craving answers. It's not easy asking such questions, but at times it seems to be a need for each of us. It is important to ask the tough questions even though we know there are no perfect answers. Life does not fit into neat little categories where everything that happens has a simplistic explanation. The Bible is not an answer book which holds precise instructions for every circumstance. It yields its wisdom to people of faith who have made a commitment to God's kind of life.

Christian people also have questions about unanswerable mysteries. We live in a wild, raw, unfinished world which stretches our imagination and calls for our best spiritual and mental energy. With God as our guide we can walk through the valley of troubled times, but the journey will not be without its anxiety. Our inability to know all there is to know and to do all there is to do about a given situation is cause for many tough questions.

The positive side of this issue is that our struggle with the unexplainable keeps us humble and dependent on God. Our inability to cope with every crisis helps us accept our human status. We turn to Him who is the author and finisher of our faith. Our ability to ask the tough questions and wrestle with life's perplexities is what salvation is all about. Only those who yearn for a Savior will find Him. In doing so, we discover that what is less than perfect can be loved as though it were perfect. While perfect answers may never come, relief does come in leaning on the everlasting arms.

- SIXTY-EIGHT -
THE JAIL OF JEALOUSY

Jealousy is a terrible curse on the human personality. It has a devastating effect upon our self-opinions. Jealousy arises out of a deep dissatisfaction with who we are and what we have. It keeps us searching endlessly for that which we think can make us complete. When we see what we think we want and someone else has it, we resent the fact that somehow life has denied us and favored another. It's a terrible way to live because we never know the joy of contentment.

A good relationship with others is often hindered because we are continually in competition with anyone who has what we want. Friendships are fractured at the slightest hint we are losing ground in the race to be most successful. Fellowship with the Father is affected by our need to test His willingness to get us what we want. We often blame God for our lagging status, since our egos are ill-equipped to accept any personal fault for our lot in life.

Jealousy is a subtle sin which, even if detected, we find difficult to confess. None of us wants to admit we are jealous, yet it is one of our most obvious weaknesses. Because who we are, what we do, and what we have consumes so much of us, our jealousies cannot be completely hidden. They become a part of our personality as they determine the tone of our behavior. We may think that jealousy is a minor flaw in our humanity, but in reality it furnishes much of the fuel for every sin in our lives. To honestly analyze our most devious iniquities is to discover the far-reaching effects of our jealous nature.

Our only hope out of this jail of jealousy in which we often find ourselves incarcerated is to seek the mind of Christ. Our Lord taught us by word and deed that self-worth is determined more by what we give up than what we get. Once we move from self to sacrifice, jealousy loses much of its power over us. When our competitive spirits give way to a genuine hunger and thirst for righteousness, we lose our need to feel superior toward anyone. The cross of Jesus becomes not only a symbol of our faith but a lesson on how to find our lives by losing them.

Jealousy does not have to dominate our disposition if the servanthood of Jesus is our model. In the development of our own servanthood, we may learn to like ourselves enough to like those of whom we have been jealous.

- SIXTY-NINE -
TAMING THE TONGUE

The discipline of speech is a prerequisite for all of us who aspire to live godly lives. What we say and how we say it is a window to our souls. Our words have a powerful capacity for either good or evil. By our speech we can redeem, and by our speech we can destroy.

Because we communicate what is within us, discipline of thought precedes discipline of talk. How quickly we say an unkind word simply because we have not considered its consequences. What thoughtless gossip we spread like garbage on the beautiful lawns of other people's lives. It is a matter of integrity that we put our minds in gear before we let our motormouths start running.

Most times, spontaneous outbursts of emotional debate reveal deep-seated anger rather than our best thoughts on an issue. Without verbal discipline in our confrontation with others, we tend to exaggerate. We use entirely too many "never" and "always" statements. We often push a point to its illogical conclusion. Even the tone of our voices indicates the lack of word control.

There is really no virtue in saying what is on our minds if indeed there is nothing of substance on our minds. One of our hardest lessons to learn is that it is not always necessary to tell others what we think. Unsolicited criticisms and pushy opinions are often obnoxious and have a high risk factor for conflict. Most folks have their own opinions of those who never have an unexpressed opinion.

As we bring our manner of speaking under control, we move closer to the character of Christ. "A soft answer turns away wrath," declared the wisdom writer. The taming of the tongue gives us a pleasant disposition for both friendship and fellowship. We tend to gravitate toward people whose kind and caring conversation gives us a sense of hope. Perhaps our most worthy spiritual ambition is that we "talk the talk" as well as "walk the walk" of the Spirit-controlled life.

Our witness is never more effective than when the "words of our mouths and the meditations of our hearts" find their inspiration in God. In no way can we be cantankerous in our talk if we allow Jesus to rule our hearts. When we do speak in haste, as often we can, our sensitive hearts will rebuke our unruly tongues.

Our prayer to God is that He touch our lips with a live coal from His altar so that we may speak with authority without being authoritarian, with love without being mushy, with courtesy without being passive, and with conviction without being judgmental. We are blessed indeed when we develop the gift of disciplined conversation.

- SEVENTY -
ESCAPE THE GLOOM

Sadness is a strange and awkward companion that travels with all of us from time to time. It attaches itself to us with devastating effects upon our outward appearance. Our somber countenance is a dead giveaway that we have been invaded by an unhappy circumstance. We cannot always hide the mood of sadness behind artificial smiles and forced optimism. It cuts deep into the heart of who we are and eventually affects everything we say and do.

Sadness is the culprit that causes us to miss out on life's happiest moments. It takes over our emotions and completely immobilizes our ability to laugh. How sad when sorrow and gloom become the dominant ingredients of our disposition.

We live in a day that spreads sadness with ever increasing effectiveness. We are inundated with news from the media that focuses upon the tragic, the destructive, and the evil aspects of our society. As a population of people drawn to the bizarre and the unusual, we thrive more on bad news than on good news. Bad news tends to be more dramatic and sells more newspapers and magazines. Good news seems tame and uneventful when shock and horror are the only things that will get our adrenalin flowing.

No wonder we are basically a sad society. Our

steady diet of gloomy information makes a demoralizing contribution to the unhealthiness and unhappiness of our inner being. No wonder drugs and alcohol are used in excess. It is the only way some folk feel they can cope with the deep, deep sadness of their souls.

Most of us have any number of ways to escape the feelings of loneliness that grip our souls. We work ourselves to exhaustion. We play ourselves silly. We travel ourselves dizzy. All of this and more simply to escape the trail of sadness that follows us like a plague.

Our greatest need, however, is not escape, but a legitimate way to resolve our inner gloom. Simon Peter, one of our Lord's dear friends, comes to our rescue by advising us to cast all our anxiety on Jesus because He cares for us. The hymn writer tells us to "take it to the Lord in prayer." He who was a man of sorrow and acquainted with grief understands the depth of our sadness. We can spread our stories of despair before Him, no matter how awkwardly expressed, and know He cares for us.

No sadness is too trite and no grief is too exaggerated that our Lord will not hear us. There is no fear of rejection because our Lord Himself extends the invitation by saying, "Come unto me, all you who labor and are heavy laden, and I will give you rest."

- SEVENTY-ONE -
JUST HUMAN

A great lesson that almost every Christian needs to learn is that it is all right to be human. Now this does not mean it is all right to be sinful. Sometimes we get the two confused as we minimize our sins by the fact that we are "just human." We use the safety net of human frailty to rationalize our weaknesses. We almost blame God for our character flaws rather than assume any personal responsibility for our misdeeds.

It is a theological and moral error to make our God-given humanity the scapegoat for all our transgressions. The truth of the matter is that being human and being sinful are not necessarily synonymous. Being human means it is all right not to know all the answers. It is all right to admit our spiritual weaknesses. It is all right to cry. It is all right to lean on each other for support. It is all right to confess our sins and seek forgiveness from God and whomever we may have offended.

Being human means that it is all right to lean on the everlasting arms of God and to resign as general manager of the universe. In fact, it is without question "more right" to be human, because the structure of our human personality cannot stand the strain of trying to play God. No doubt, we sin more in our attempt to be God than in our struggle with being human. We have far too much to learn about the dynamics of our own humanity before we begin taking lessons in the art of being divine.

Yet we seem to be incurably possessed with the need to hate, to condemn, and to return evil for evil. We are forever trying to improve on what we perceive to be "God's creative blunders" as we seek to re-create everyone in our own image. Everyone who does not have our brand of spirituality and religious disposition is the object of our concern and sometimes the object of our scorn.

Our greatest need may be that we relax our ambition to be judges and umpires of each other's lives. There is great relief when we grow to understand that "vengeance is mine, I will repay, saith the Lord." After all, being human means that we understand our common plight. We struggle to forgive and forget. We learn to be healers instead of agitators. Somewhere along life's journey we begin to accept our servant role as the best expression of our humanity.

- SEVENTY-TWO -
BE NOT AFRAID

Fear is one of the most traumatic aspects of our human emotions. It can create a disposition which alters our personality and produces a mood of despair. Sometimes fear is a temporary response to some crisis, and again it may become a behavior pattern. Most people experience fear from time to time while others live a life of fear.

Some fear is normal and healthy. Constant fear is a tragic state of existence with all kinds of emotional and spiritual consequences. Such fear is a cancer of the soul that eats away at our capacity to believe and trust. It is the selfish preoccupation with our own needs and hurts. It is the inability to feel nothing but self-pity and remorse over life's difficulties.

Fear is a problem with which we all must deal because of the many unknown factors about life. Sometimes it seems that our ability for fear is greater than our ability for faith. Our deep desire is to believe in God and His ability to see us through, but fear often separates us from the power that can redeem us.

How, then, do we cope with life's paralyzing fears? Paul, in writing to young Timothy, said, "God has not given us the spirit of fear; but of power, and of love, and of a sound mind." Here is one way of dealing with our fear. According to Paul, fear is not of

God. If it is not of God, then it must be of self and sin. Therefore, it is appropriate to repent of our fear and seek the power, the love, and the mind of God.

The psalmist promised God, "What time I am afraid I will trust in Thee." He saw trust as a redeeming factor in the midst of life's fearful circumstances. He was unwilling to allow fear to gain control of his emotions. The psalmist recognized the reality of fear, yet he refused to give it a predominant place in his life. He used fear to motivate his trust in God rather than as a means of destroying his ability to believe.

We learn from both Paul and the psalmist that fear only frightens us when we give it that power. Perhaps it is true that in Christ Jesus we have nothing to fear but fear itself. Therefore, as we walk through the troubled waters of our lives, let us listen for the voice of our Master, who once spoke to His fearful disciples, "Be of good cheer; it is I; be not afraid."

- SEVENTY-THREE -
UNLOCK YOUR DOOR

The latch on the door to her heart was firmly fastened. There were years of disappointment kept tightly secured within her inner being. Memories were too painful to mess with. She punished herself daily for the sins of the past. Some were her own and some belonged to others. In a sordid kind of way she clung to her weaknesses as an excuse for being a loner. She rejected most people because of the mistreatment by a few. She respected no one because she had little respect for herself. It was too risky to have close friends who might try to pry open the door to her heart.

She was a beautiful person, but she did not know it. She constantly guarded the unacceptable person she thought was hiding somewhere within her subconscious. She would not let light shine into the dark cellar of her own self-image. The mistruths and mistreatment of others caused her to doubt her own sanity. She internalized everyone's behavior and at times enjoyed the role of martyr. Her door was shut and sealed, but the Savior kept knocking and saying, "Behold, I stand at the door and knock. If you will open I will come in and eat with you."

He was a macho man. The door to his heart was also closed. He enjoyed the male role in life. He took pride in his manliness, but it was a front. Deep inside he was afraid and lonely. He too had been hurt, but he was too "brave" to admit it. He could not afford to let others think there were cracks in his armor. When he allowed himself to cry (in total privacy) he was ashamed of his weakness. The need to be in control caused him to boast. The need always to be right made him defensive. He needed to talk to someone, but who would understand? There was a little boy inside who needed to escape, but he would not release him.

People looked up to him because they thought he was someone he was not. He looked down on himself because he knew he was not who they thought he was. Underneath his macho exterior was a kind and gentle person, but he would not let himself see this. The door to his heart was barricaded by many misconceptions of real manhood. The Savior kept knocking and saying, "Behold, I stand at the door and knock. If you will open I will come in and eat with you."

Stop! Listen! There is a faint sound outside. Someone is knocking at your heart. It is Jesus. He is the only One who needs to come into your inner sanctum. The latch, however, is on the inside.

- SEVENTY-FOUR -
SECRET HIDEAWAY

There is a lonely place to which hurting people sometimes go. It is called "withdrawal." They go thinking they have found a safe haven from their woes. They wrap themselves in an emotional cocoon as a cushion against their pain. They internalize their grief and often get locked into a rut of only one way of thinking. Their imaginations play tricks on them as they lose touch with reality. Many times withdrawal causes folk to lash out at those who love them most and could care for them best. It is not easy dealing with life's complications, but retreating within oneself does not make it easier. People who turn inward to lick their own wounds have a limited source of healing.

Living with loneliness is a pain our Lord does not wish us to have. His invitation in times of despair is quite obvious. His friendship is as close to us as our ability to pray and seek His face. His word becomes our comfort, His presence becomes our strength, and His promises become our hope.

Whenever we tend to withdraw He wants to share our inner feelings. He wants to correct and caress our awkward thoughts. Because He is a man of sorrows and acquainted with grief, He understands the deepest wounds of our broken hearts. If we invite Him into the secret hideaway of our souls, He will help us keep our perspective. He will not remove the possibility of pain, but He will guide us through its adventure.

Of course, there is value in withdrawal if we understand the dynamics of our loneliness. Being alone can give us time to sort through our thoughts. It can give us a humble and contrite heart. The silence of our soul is a time for God to speak to us. On several occasions Jesus had to withdraw from the crowds in order to have time with God the Father. It was a constructive retreat from public scrutiny and clamoring demands upon His time. He came back with renewed energy for His Messianic assignments.

Our Lord is a good model of mixing our public and private needs. We must never get so public that we lose our depth of concentration. Neither should we become so private that loneliness conquers our happiness. May our symptoms of withdrawal be occasions for hearing His still small voice.

- SEVENTY-FIVE -
MEMORIES FOR THE FUTURE

Sometimes we find ourselves wishing things could be the way they were, but "the way they were" did not last very long. Whatever past circumstances we long for were temporary at best. Nostalgia is a fickle feeling. It can give us pleasant thoughts about days gone by, and yet it can cause us to be so unrealistic about the past that we penalize our present and our future.

Time moves on and change is inevitable. The "good old days" are but a memory of a time when we thought we had less stress and strain. We tend to forget the complications of life back then because present complications overshadow anything that ever has been. In an attempt to escape the painful perplexities of today we try to reconstruct yesterday according to how we wish it had been.

Even though things never were exactly the way we think they were, we must never stop making beautiful memories. It may be out of the way we think things were that we find the motivation to create a tomorrow in the way we want it to be. In this manner our memories are closely connected to our dreams. Perhaps the only way we can construct our dreams is by remembering the way we wish things had been.

Therefore, as we long for the good old days, we

can actually prepare ourselves for a better new day if we understand that every day has its share of hopes and horrors. The key is to be realistically aware that today we are making memories for the future. Yesterday is but a reminder that today contains the ingredients for a healthier tomorrow.

The major focus of our lives needs to be on the present. It is the only time we have. We cannot honestly reconstruct the past nor can we accurately produce the future. "Today is the day of salvation. Now is the accepted time." Forgiveness and grace as well as beautiful memories enable us to live with our past. The kind of hope that produces a positive attitude enables us to move graciously into the future. It is the disposition of the present moment that controls our appraisal of both.

Let us, therefore, never minimize this present breath of life, this existing heartbeat of love, and this moment of consciousness. Indeed, the psalmist gave us great insight when he wrote, "This is the day the Lord has made. We will rejoice and be glad in it."

BENEDICTION

O Lord my God, You are a mighty being. I celebrate Your creative ingenuity. I marvel at the mystery of Your ways and the power by which You perform Your purpose.

You have made me with a capacity to be curious and for that reason I am filled with wonder and awe. My eager imagination causes me to reflect upon how it was in the beginning. From my limited human perspective, I imagine You busying Yourself with creation's chores. I can see You flinging stars, moon and sun into their places and putting planets into their orbits as You decorate the heavens for centuries of celestial observation.

In my mind's eye, I see You selecting planet earth as a special garden to express the beauty of Your creative skills. I observe You spinning it around the sun in such a way that its seasons offer heat and health for all kinds of living things. I see You setting in motion a variety of laws and principles which my most scientific thoughts have yet to grasp. I imagine You calling forth all the elements of earth and arranging them in geometric continuity. I see You looking out over Your created order and You are pleased.

The beauty which my imagination is able to behold is limited only by my lack of vision. I stop short of seeing ultimate reality because sin and time have dulled my senses.

As I watch You moving amid that which You have made, I detect a note of loneliness. You have no one with whom to share Your marvelous universe. I wonder what is going through Your mind. And then I see You bend over and tenderly form a bit of dust into Your own image. You breathe into that lifeless form the breath of life and it becomes a living being. A smile comes across Your face and then a sense of sadness. You have created humankind who can give You delight but may also give You grief. You are God and You are Glory. I praise You because I am wonderfully made.

But who am I that You are mindful of me? Who am I to have the benefit of Your inspired thoughts? Who am I to deserve this breath of life and this moment of grace? Who am I to think I could even imagine creation's mystery? I want to be Your humble servant who longs not only to dream about You, but to dream with You.

May my thoughts before You give me a power surge for future challenges. Amen.